ADAPTED FROM THE U.S.
MILITARY'S
IN HUM
TE

INNOVATIVE, NON-TRADITIONAL
MANAGEMENT SKILLS
TO GIVE YOU...

THE WARRIOR'S EDGE

"A powerful statement on both the need and the techniques to attain high levels of personal excellence."

Sen. Claiborne Pell

"Thought-provoking... New concepts from the Human Potential movement... Gives new meaning to 'be all that you can be.'"

Dr. H.E. Puthoff, Institute for Advanced Studies

"The cutting edge of the human psyche, new and old powers of mind, applied with the discipline and abandon of Bushido."

Jim Morris, author of *War Story*

"Reveals that there definitely is enormous power in techniques that have yet to be explained by science. In the meantime, we can use them to win."

Dr. Bob Wood, McDonnell Douglas Space Systems

THE WARRIOR'S EDGE

FRONT-LINE STRATEGIES FOR VICTORY ON THE CORPORATE BATTLEFIELD

COLONEL JOHN B. ALEXANDER,
MAJOR RICHARD GROLLER & JANET MORRIS

AVON BOOKS ◆ NEW YORK

AVON BOOKS
A division of
The Hearst Corporation
1350 Avenue of the Americas
New York, New York 10019

Copyright © 1990 by Paradise Productions
Published by arrangement with William Morrow and Company, Inc.
Library of Congress Catalog Card Number: 90-5794
ISBN: 0-380-71674-7

The William Morrow and Company edition contains the following Library of Congress Cataloging in Publication Data:

Alexander, John B.
   The warrior's edge / John B. Alexander, Richard Groller, Janet Morris.
      p.   cm.
   Includes bibliographical references.
   1. Parapsychology.   2. Parapsychology—Military aspects.
I. Groller, Richard.   II. Morris, Janet, 1946–   .   II. Title.
BF1031.A42
133./8—dc20   90-5794
                                                                    CIP

First Avon Books Printing: June 1992

Printed in the U.S.A.

OPM   10   9   8   7   6   5   4   3   2   1

ACKNOWLEDGMENTS

Over the course of time, many have assisted in discovering and developing *The Warrior's Edge*. Some of them cannot be named here. They know who they are and we thank each of them.

Several people have participated actively in the gathering of material for this book and to these we extend our heartfelt gratitude: Robert Jahn and Brenda Dunne at Princeton University; Jack Houck; Hal Puthoff; Jim Hardt; Foster Gamble; David Shanahoff-Khalsa; and Bob Klaus.

General Maxwell Thurman (U.S. Army) allowed the human technology task force to be formed. His support was invaluable.

Special thanks goes to Major General Albert N. Stubblebine, U.S. Army (Ret.), without whom this book would never have been written. He had both the foresight and the fortitude to support our studies, for which he paid a great price.

Chris Morris was an unheralded, invaluable partner in this project from its inception. He consulted throughout, edited draft manuscript, contributed chapter titles, initial paragraphs, and exercises that helped make this book the best it could be.

Acknowledgments

Perry Knowlton, our agent, read and critiqued drafts of the proposal material until it met his standard.

Tony Gardner counseled Janet and Chris Morris at this project's most critical stage and we owe him a great deal.

Tish Groller helped edit crucial chapters and gave us unflagging moral, intellectual, and even physical support.

Dave Quast, at the Aviation Week & Space Technology Library, solved a seemingly insoluble problem for us.

Dr. Jan Northup hosted our start-up meeting, giving freely of her stress-management expertise, as well as her hospitality.

Finally, we would like to thank Adrian Zackheim and his team at William Morrow for their impressive performance. Adrian's skill, vision, and enthusiasm kept everyone on track. Pamela Altschul was continually generous with her acuity and her time. Veronica Windholz, our copy editor, worked wonders for us.

CONTENTS

8

Contents

INTRODUCTION

The age of human excellence and optimum performance is dawning, according to experts in the U.S. and other Western, as well as Soviet/Eastern European governments. Extraordinary results are being realized through research into human technology around the world. Human optimization is becoming a trainable skill.

Using techniques developed by government and civilian researchers from the United States to the Soviet Union, anyone can learn to develop and employ the extraordinary capabilities latent in each human being.

The Warrior's Edge maps this hidden realm, for so long terra incognita. This guide is a manual for exploring, training, and using the innate abilities within the human body/mind system, abilities long misunderstood, denied, and ignored by modern societies.

The purpose of this book is to unlock the door to the extraordinary human potentials inherent in each of us. To do this, we, like governments around the world, must take a fresh look at nontraditional methods of affecting reality. We must raise human consciousness of the potential power of the individual body/

mind system—the power to manipulate reality. We must be willing to retake control of our past, present and, ultimately, our future.

When shorn of spiritualism and trained by scientific method, the shaman of the past becomes the techno-shaman of today, a psychic warrior capable of using the tools of science to reveal the secrets hidden within the human mind.

To unlock these secrets, to understand and manipulate humanity's connection with the universe, one must first shed popular preconceptions and misconceptions. We will warn you that this book is not for the dogmatic: Disbelief is a self-fulfilling prophecy and a prerequisite for failure when dealing with the powers of the mind. It is an axiom of mental training that you get what you expect. To get the most out of this book, expect to be challenged, expect to be excited, expect to be a more effective human being when your training is done. For if you expect to fail, your mind will deliver that result.

If, however, you maintain an open mind, the untapped potential locked within you can be realized by study and training. You can employ the same techniques used by researchers and project managers around the world to improve your performance and control more of your mind and your reality.

Because this is a book about human potential, the nature of reality, and "psychic" phenomena, we will present a new perspective, showing how psychic phenomena fit into a quantum-mechanical model of reality. The misnomer *psychic* is particularly unfortunate, given the number of tricksters and charlatans who have appropriated it, because psychic, or psi, potentials are within the grasp of everyone. If an individual realizes that these phenomena are not unnatural, the work of the devil, or the province of social deviants, the results of this training can be a greater confidence, a more effective and integrated sense of self, and dominion over a wide range of human experience.

In the Soviet Union/Eastern European countries, the all-encompassing term *psychotronics* is used to categorize many phenomena currently subject to scientific research. Within the category of psychotronics, the Russians identify as biocommunications the following discrete skills:

bioinformation: *telepathy* (using the human mind to tap into the thoughts of others)

remote viewing (to see or otherwise monitor events occurring at a distant location)

bioenergetics: *psychokinesis* (PK—altering or affecting molecular states)

All these phenomena involve using the mind and/or some "field" of the body to affect other minds and inanimate objects, sometimes at a distance, without the intervention of conventional mechanisms such as electronics or tools. We will discuss the methods researchers are using to document these types of abilities and show how a person can, through training, acquire these skills.

Of all the categories listed above, one of the most useful and interesting is remote viewing, sometimes called remote perception or remote sensing. Remote viewing allows a practitioner to acquire information irrespective of intervening distance—or elapsed time. This capability has obvious intelligence-gathering potential, and studies at Stanford Research Institute, as well as other research, verify its usefulness. Think of what it would be like to be able to learn, in advance, what a competitor or an ally is thinking or to know the plans or state of mind of another person, even if that person is half a world away. Other governments have.

It is well documented that the Soviet Union and its allies have invested millions of dollars in psychotronics, using as their basic premise: We believe that something exists that has no normal, rational explanation—let us investigate it.

The U.S., on the other hand, has fallen as much as twenty years behind the U.S.S.R., some analysts believe. The reason for this is the widely held view of Western scientists: First prove to me that it exists, then I'll believe it.

This dogmatism has all but stifled publicly funded U.S. research. Legitimate research has continued, however quietly, despite a climate of scientific elitism in which investigators risk ridicule and loss of credibility in the scientific community.

This closed-minded attitude causes political difficulties when presenting psychic research to the scientific community. Consequently, relentless diligence is demanded of those applying scientific methods to the area of psychotronics.

Thus the experimental methods used in psi research today are as rigid as those required by other sciences. This, and the fact that a great deal of the psychotronic work being done is classified by the various foreign governments involved, has resulted in a curtain of ignorance that obscures from the public eye many valuable and exciting results of psychic research.

In the following chapters, we will outline ways to increase human potential using techniques explored by the U.S. Army in its Jedi Project, which sought to construct teachable models of behavioral/physical excellence using unconventional means. The results will improve your performance in any area to which these methods are applied.

Additionally, we include exercises for heightening sensory awareness and expanding the limits of consciousness. We will also present theories of how and why these techniques produce results in the physical world.

This book is primarily devoted to practice, not theory. We know these techniques work; the physics that underlie these phenomena are beginning to take comprehensible shape. But you no more need to understand the quantum-mechanical bases for psychic phenomena than you need to understand the workings of an internal combustion engine in order to start your car. The ways and means to practice, learn, control, and apply psychotronic techniques are available to us now, in this book.

Humans have evolved over millennia, and yet the most dramatic increases in the scope of human knowledge have occurred within the last century. Our current knowledge base is expanding exponentially. As a result of so much new information, we are beginning to realize how little we do know—and how much of what we thought we knew, even a few years ago, has proved false.

Like fire, psi has been used since the dawn of recorded history, until now with little understanding of its nature. The tools for its measurement are finally being developed. The tools for its use lie within the human "biosystem": your body, your mind, your concentration, your will.

We will show, in our discussion of the Jedi Project, that human willpower and human concentration affect performance more than any other single factor. We will discuss the role of expectation in performance and examine the axiom "You get what you expect."

We will discuss reality and an individual's place in it. We will present the thesis that two levels of reality—objective and subjective—exist and that both are susceptible to the trained mind. Your subjective reality already understands psychotronics; your objective reality needs only to be convinced, and trained to admit the data your own psychic system—your body/mind transceiver—collects.

Because the way a person views reality defines the limits and boundaries of not only an individual world view but of individual achievement, being able to alter these paradigms can have profound results.

Quantum mechanics considers the influence of the observer on the observation and calls that interaction causality. There is no reason *not* to believe that consciousness has an affect upon the surrounding environment; there is no place free of the influence of the observer where measurements could be made that would refute this statement.

The laws of physics are still evolving. Physics is meeting metaphysics, putting forth such concepts as advance potential waves, which are perceived before they are generated and thus are an example of an effect that occurs before its cause. Electrons are penetrating barriers that, by all the laws of probability, should be impenetrable. Scientists are beginning to speak of the

Dirac Sea, a limitless expanse of energy comprising the interconnected fabric of the universe.

It is this interconnection of the universe that we will explore. We will show you how researchers are liberating the full potential of the human being. We will usher you into a world where time itself need not be a barrier to the human mind—where your past, your present, and your future are more amenable to your control than you once thought possible.

Only the multidisciplined warrior, the techno-shaman, can scale the walls of ignorance and shed light over the prevailing darkness. The warrior spirit must guide this process. So we will teach you how to become warriors in the spirit, as well as the physical, realm.

The tools you need to embark on the path of discovery are in your hands. The discipline required is the discipline of the open mind. That discipline is at the heart of what we call the warrior's edge.

The three of us wish you a safe and successful journey beyond the boundaries of everyday experience. Each of us has, at one time or another, bet his life on the skills we call the warrior's edge and lived to talk about it. For every anecdote recounted in these pages, there are dozens we can't tell. But we are practitioners of what we preach.

John Alexander evolved from hard-core mercenary to thanatologist, obtaining his doctorate under the direction of Dr. Elisabeth Kübler-Ross. In 1956 he entered the U.S. Army as a private and retired thirty-two years later as a colonel. As a Special Forces A-Team commander in Thailand and Vietnam, he led hundreds of mercenaries into battle. At the same time, he studied meditation in Buddhist monasteries and later engaged in technical exploration and demonstration of advanced human performance. He was chief of the Advanced Human Technology Office, U.S. Army Intelligence and Security Command; and director, Advanced Systems Concepts Office, U.S. Army Laboratory Command. As such, he provided advice to the National Research Council for its study *Enhancing Human Performance*.

Introduction

Richard Groller (Major, USAR), exemplifies the modern-day techno-shaman. A military intelligence officer in the U.S. Army for over eleven years, Rich is a mathematician, MBA, and systems engineer. On active duty, he served in a variety of high-tech, R&D, and operational assignments on the staffs of the Directorate of Intelligence, U.S. Forces Command, the 7th Infantry Division, and the U.S. Army Intelligence School. A student of the paranormal for almost twenty years and a scientist concerned with the physics underlying psychic phenomena, Rich was nominated for Military Intelligence Professional Writer of the Year for his investigation of Soviet military research in parapsychology.

Janet Morris is the author or editor of more than thirty books, many of which have been published abroad in British, German, Italian, French, and Japanese editions. Elected to the New York Academy of Sciences in 1980, she is affiliated with the National Intelligence Study Center. In 1972–3, she worked on a research project investigating the effect of mind on probability in computer systems. The problems of geochronometry—a mathematical approach to philosophical problems of space and time—raised by that study led her to subsequent hands-on investigations: She was initiated into the Japanese art of bioenergetics, joh re, the Indonesian brotherhood of Subud, and graduated from the Silva course in advanced mind control. She has been doing remote viewing for fifteen years.

All of us have successfully used our warrior's edge not only to survive in life-threatening situations but to win hearts and minds, to motivate ourselves and others, and to exceed "normal" limits of performance. We believe this book can put that advantage in your hands. We hope it will serve you well.

1
BELIEVERS

Inherent in the makeup of each human mind is a belief system. The warrior has a belief system; so does the mother, the physician, the scientist . . . and so do you.

Your belief system, evolving over your lifetime, orders your entire physical and cognitive experience. It absorbs, collates, and evaluates all lessons, from cultural mores to intellectual truths proven by personal experience.

From infancy, we collect, correlate, and learn to transmit sensory data. The sum of these impressions make up our mind's internal model of the reality around us. With maturity, *value judgments* replace sensory data as primary factors determining our regard for someone or some thing.

As we mature, we often consciously alter our beliefs, usually because experience teaches us that some long-held beliefs are no longer valid. In so doing, we are recognizing the fact that our beliefs mold our personal realities—our lives—and acting on that information to make our lives better.

Our success in life, in our own eyes, is dependent on our success in this endeavor. Each person's model of reality is unique and defines that individual in no uncertain terms, yet shared belief systems are the heart of such concepts as patriotism, nationalism, religion, philosophy, and politics. Shared belief systems are the drivers that politicians use to pass laws and national leaders use to declare wars.

Shared belief systems are powerful. The belief system to which you subscribe may dictate the way you live or even the way you die.

The warrior's belief system clearly defines how life should be lived and death should be approached. If a warrior is "not one who goes to war or kills people, but rather one who exhibits integrity in his actions and control over his life,"[1] what then does the warrior believe?

The warrior knows that evil cannot be overcome in this lifetime; it can only be resisted within oneself. Therefore, the warrior remains objective in all situations—the observer, prepared to act on matters of conscience. The warrior strives to separate truth from perception when the two are at odds; to stand firm in conviction, even when doing so runs counter to popular thought.

The struggle to support the values of true warriorship is difficult. Rarely are situations right or wrong; frequently, the need to act is accompanied by imprecise information on which to base decisions. Yet the warrior must act—with the purpose of balancing the scales, not out of vengeance. The act is well thought out, even if performed almost simultaneously. The warrior selectively chooses when to act: As Confucius said, "The superior man fights only great battles."

The key attributes of the warrior are *will* and *patience*. One of the principles of military leadership is to "know yourself and seek self-improvement."[2] Will and patience, essential to this task, are the motivating forces at the warrior's core.

The warrior acts decisively and strategically while seeking self-mastery and self-awareness, continually conscious that life is fragile and death waits at the end of it.

What tenets shape the warrior's beliefs?

Moral courage: a stringent code that values honor and struggle for a cause.

Willingness to risk: The warrior knows he may not always win; he is prepared to spend his life for his beliefs.

Devotion: The warrior chooses a noble cause that instills in him devotion to duty and serves the human family.

Decisiveness: the ability to recognize correct action, take that action, and accept responsibility denotes a warrior.

The warrior "aims to follow his heart, to choose consciously the items that make up his world, to be exquisitely aware of everything around him, to attain total control, then act with total abandon. He seeks in short, to live an impeccable life."[3]

If only in our dreams, all men and women are striving for true warriorship. To attain it, one must understand the warrior psyche and put its tenets into action in one's life: You must examine your belief system.

Layers of belief are stratified and hierarchical. They may include religion, cultural bias, or political views—all you hold to be unshakably true.

THE BELIEF-SYSTEM TREE

Let us imagine that your belief system is a tree. The roots of your tree lie beneath the surface. From them you draw sustenance and determine your sense of "place" in the world.

Your evaluation over time of these root processes shapes the growth of your belief-system tree. The feelings you draw from your root level become certainties: trusted, reliable strategies for solving problems—beliefs in action, each feeding the tree an assimilated experience.

Beliefs held at the root level include your collection of firsts—those initial, lasting, often nonverbal impressions of hot, cold, sharp, smooth, good, lonely, safe. Such root impressions color our whole belief tree and may keep us from investigating areas labeled frightening, shocking, or dangerous. These are precisely the areas that you, an evolving personality, must review occasionally, to make sure you are living life fully.

Don't be afraid to "expose your roots," at least to yourself. You must inventory your roots to prune or nurture needy areas.

Outmoded behavior patterns should be cut away, along with beliefs that experience has proved erroneous. New root growth will emerge to feed the maturing tree. These new roots will be superior, pliant, and more nurturing due to their improved link to actual external conditions.

This root-level evaluation and vetting of beliefs allows new thought patterns, sometimes new pathways in the brain, to develop. Confirmed, reliable, accurate observations of reality comprise the fundament that supports and feeds your belief-system tree. Just as an ornamental horticulturist sculpts the growth of a bonsai tree, you can sculpt your mind's development. The goals you set are directly proportional to the amount of faith you have in yourself.

THE MECHANICS OF BELIEF

Beliefs are often strongly held, even in the face of massive contradictory evidence. Max Planck, physicist and Nobel laureate, remarked that new beliefs [in science] aren't made by the strength of fact, but rather that the old order dies out and, with it, its outdated ideas.

The military, too, has its old order. Many military organizations are conservative by nature and slow to change. Yet the military traditionally searches out and tests new and alternative techniques. The brighter military minds have always been aware of the effects of new technologies and tactics on the battlefield. The long bow, the tank, and the atomic bomb are examples of technologies that have rapidly transformed the nature of warfare.

During the American Revolution, we learned that hiding and shooting was better than lining up and marching across an open field. Nevertheless, we returned to the older, more conservative tactics throughout the Civil War. Shaka Zulu conquered most of southern Africa by adapting the strategy of closing with and destroying his enemies. Prior to that, the opposing forces mostly yelled and attempted to intimidate each other.

We fear technological surprise by our adversaries. Scientists in the defense industry explore many areas in hopes that weapons systems may be developed using unexpected approaches. We need to be equally zealous in discovering ways to improve human performance.

In this book we present ideas that many of the old order may be hesitant to accept. Still, there is sufficient evidence supporting these theses to warrant examination.

One would be naive to assume that we know all we need to know about the universe, the physical world, or ourselves. As Planck said, "Modern physics impresses us particularly with the truth of the old doctrine which teaches that there are realities existing apart from our sense perceptions, and that there are problems and conflicts where these realities are of greater value for us than the richest treasure of world experience."[4]

Some of what you will experience in this book may challenge your current belief system. We do not ask you to change your beliefs. What we do ask is that you experiment with the techniques and, if they work for you, by all means use them.

Psychologists use the term *cognitive dissonance* to describe the stress engendered when one behaves in a fashion counter to one's beliefs. Such stress is a signal that belief and behavior are at odds and it is time to make a choice: Forgo the behavior or change your beliefs. If no stress occurs, a technique is not antithetical to your personal belief system.

There is an old saying, "Seeing is believing," that is increasingly contradicted by the marvels of innovative technology. Things we see today may not necessarily exist outside a computer simulation. Computer-graphics programs have already advanced to a point where, in many courts in the United States, photographs are no longer admissible as evidence. And, although our system of jurisprudence still places a great deal of faith and confidence in eyewitness accounts, such testimony often proves unreliable.

The common problem here is not lying witnesses but witnesses whose perceptions are clouded by their belief system— who juxtapose a preferred reality over actual events. Often, people see what they expect to see. A classic example of this is the following picture (figure 1), which can be interpreted as either a young woman or an old hag.[5]

Try this little exercise. Read the following statement and quickly count the number of letter *f*'s that you see:

Throughout all of recorded history principles of living have been firmly established and one of the oldest is that future actions

Figure 1

of each individual are unfailingly determined by the current thoughts of that individual."

The correct answer is eight. Did you miss any? It is quite common not to count the *f* in each of the *of*s in the sentence. This occurs not because they are hidden but because the mind concentrates on the longer words.

The psychological term to describe this phenomenon is *scotoma*. Literally, your mind fills in the blanks and you see what you *expect* to see, *overlaid* on what is really there. This same phenomenon exists in our daily lives.

Your beliefs color everything you survey; awareness of them allows you to reflect, to consciously tune your internal biases, and to make reasoned decisions in light of them. Or, if you choose, to change those biases.

We've all heard the saying "love is blind." Many of us have even joined the ranks of the "sightless" once or twice in our lives. Reason cast aside, we act upon our perceptions of the moment. Later, we are left wondering how we could have been so oblivious to certain negative traits in the person we once thought perfect.

Denial is one of the mind's most powerful tools. Denial helps us cope with the overwhelming. It also prevents many of us from exploring our universe as it really is. People who witness tragic events often cannot remember specific details. Unpleasant incidents, although stored in the unconscious, may be consciously denied. Dr. Elisabeth Kübler-Ross describes denial as one of the major stages of the death and dying process.[6] Patients go to extreme lengths to deny that anything is physically wrong with them, deciding their tests were wrong or the results belonged to someone else.

To be effective, the warrior must maintain an open belief system. Negative or unrealistic thinking limits anyone's possibilities for success. The warrior must be able to observe his surroundings accurately and minimize the distortion of expectation and preconception. This applies collectively as well as individually.

All professional military strategists agree that surprise is one of the principles of war. Technological surprise, currently a great concern, is best prevented by keeping belief systems open. We have not always been successful at this. We were surprised by the Soviets' ability to build very large submarines with a deep-diving capability—even though HUMINT (Human Intelligence) sources reported such submarine development—because conventional wisdom said that large-hulled craft couldn't withstand the pressure encountered at operational depths. Only when actual overhead photographic reconnaissance systems caught the craft on camera did opinion change. In this case, the belief systems of closed-minded analysts impaired our ability to recognize a new threat.

BELIEF AND THE WARRIOR

The warrior's beliefs are an integral part of his arsenal. When he must, he changes his beliefs to make his performance more effective, exactly as he would discard an old weapon for a new, more capable one. He trains himself to utilize the strengths of his beliefs, exactly as he would train with a new weapon—until its use becomes second nature and its competence becomes his competence.

Belief systems are difficult to change. The more deeply held the belief, the harder it is to change. This is why we recommend *doing* the exercises, not just reading about them.

Language can play a powerful part in the change of beliefs. Sometimes changing the words used to describe an item or event can have great impact. For example, most people believe that it is wrong to kill another human being, yet we send our young off to war and expect them to rapidly change their beliefs and begin killing on command. To facilitate this change, we often use new words, commonly racist in nature, to describe the enemy. In Vietnam, we labeled the enemy *dinks*, *slopes*, and *zips*. Because words can have positive as well as negative power, we will teach you some new words for new capabilities.

Critical events can abruptly change beliefs. A classic case is that of Admiral Leahy, who said, "The [atomic] bomb will never go off, and I speak as an expert on explosives." Leahy's beliefs changed early in 1944, with the detonation of the first atomic bomb at Trinity Site, New Mexico. When the belief system of a person, a nation, or the world changes, so do expectations.

For now, we ask that you expand your belief system just enough to practice with these weapons we are offering and make them part of your arsenal, so that their use can become second nature and their competence can become your competence.

The result will be the warrior's edge.

2
MIND CONTROL

The mind never sleeps. However, our awareness of our mental functions fluctuates over a wide range. When we are asleep, tired, or under the influence of alcohol or drugs, our control of mental faculties is inarguably lessened. When we are excited, anxious, expectant, or in pain, our perceptual abilities operate at heightened levels: the survival instinct preempts all other directives.

Somewhere between unconsciousness and hyperacuity is a center position we will call your control center. You operate from your control center during most of your normal, waking daily life; you've just never named it before.

Your control center formulates and expedites strategies for enhancing your condition in the world—problem-solving strategies.

Quieting the mind brings your control center sharply into focus, allowing you to touch base with the unique and formidable array of tools and techniques you have fashioned in the forge of your personal experience.

Those operating in this new dimension must have constant and unabridged access to their control center so that even under extraordinary conditions the control center's resources are available to them. Under any circumstances, from exhaustion to exhilaration, this control center is your connection to the overwhelming abundance of life-supporting and life-preserving data you carry throughout your person. From the genetic data implanted over eons by your forebears to the infinite potential of the greatest supercomputer of them all—your brain—you can access a virtually limitless source of well-being that awaits any who will venture to the well and drink.

The well is your control center. To get there, you must practice remaining consciously in control.

Remain in control as your body drifts toward nonawareness of the physical.

Remain in control as input from your surroundings tries to intrude on your sense of calm.

Remain in control as diffuse situations coalesce into focused and manageable equations.

The first step in the mastery of the techniques that will follow is that of getting control of one's own mind. This may sound easy, but for many people it is difficult to accomplish. We are culturally accustomed to allowing our senses to be bombarded with external influences, the majority of which require some degree of mental attention.

Our society thrives on multisensory stimulation. To enhance presentations, companies employ a multimedia approach, with attractive visual displays supported by various sounds. Some presenters even insert olfactory cues to stimulate the senses. When the day is done, we drive our automobiles through frenetic rush-hour traffic; to soothe ourselves while caught in traffic, we listen to the radio. Some control their sensory input by choosing "easy listening"; some hope to be relaxed by classical music; some choose rock 'n' roll; too few choose silence. Rarely do we allow ourselves to become still enough to listen to our inner selves. In a society addicted to external stimuli, many of us have lost the ability to calm the mind or to become attuned to our inner selves.

The military, as well as most businesses, rewards individuals who thrive on chaos. The management of chaos has become an accepted way of doing business in this country. The highest form of organized chaos is, in fact, the conduct of war. A German general officer once remarked that "the reason that the American army does so well in wartime is that war is chaos, and the American army practices chaos on a daily basis."

When the Department of the Army (DA) decided to implement a stress-management program in selected parts of the DCSPER (Deputy Chief of Staff, Personnel) and DCSOPS (Deputy Chief of Staff, Operations) Staff at the Pentagon, Dr. Meyer Friedman (the author of the Type A and Type B stress-identification system) was brought in as a consulting physician. After reviewing the psychological profiles of both the control group (DCSOPS) and the stress trainees (DCSPER), he commented that he had never seen an organization so far out of balance. Type A personalities abounded.

The military tends to attract people who are aggressive by nature. The officer corps, even more so. Most officers start their careers by going to jump school and ranger school, then serving time in combat arms units (infantry, armor, or artillery). Those who do not like the competitive environment leave voluntarily at an early stage. Those who choose to stay must pass through many selection gates for promotions and schooling. By the time one enters the Pentagon, anyone who is not highly competitive by nature has either changed or been eliminated from the system.

THE FORTY-TIGER DAY

Many of you are familiar with the fight-or-flight response that occurs when you are confronted with an imminent threat to your well-being. In our ancestors, fight-or-flight response evolved as an adaptation to a physically threatening environment. In a face-to-face confrontation with a saber-toothed tiger, humans required instant reactions: You fought or you fled. Since one rarely encountered tigers on a daily basis, the body could afford to put tremendous physical effort into such a response. If you survived, you had time after the confrontation to relax.

Today, although we aren't threatened by true tigers, we continue to respond physically to stress as if confronted by a saber-toothed tiger. Executives in stressful jobs respond as if they were fighting tigers an estimated forty to fifty times per day. The body pays a significant price for maintaining this level of arousal.

Certainly, the warrior must be physically and mentally prepared to operate under extreme combat stress. The problem is that most of the time, we are *not* engaged in hostilities—yet we tend to operate as if we were. People pay a dramatic price for such behavior. Top leadership has recognized that price as contributory to the death or incapacitation of many of our emerging young leaders.

In the civilian sector, executives and managers work under high stress for long periods of time. Successful performers, in and out of government, joke about how infrequently they take vacations. Many even forfeit vacation time due to the use-or-lose vacation policies established by most firms. A growing health consciousness among the American people has helped point out the dangers, but the warning is too often unheeded.

This nearly pathological drive to excel caused Dr. Friedman to tell the DA staff that he would not take a patient unless the candidate had had one prior heart attack, because until such a dramatic event had occurred, it was futile to try getting such a person's attention.

There are exercises that can help you practice quieting your own mind in order to gain better control of your body, your sense perception and, eventually, your life-style. These same calming exercises allow you to control your response to an actual modern-day "tiger"—a real crisis—and teach you that in most instances, you will have the ability to make potential tigers disappear. The warrior first quiets his tigers by not fighting unnecessary battles and then by fighting with the power of all the techniques at his disposal. To do this, you must be particularly aware of the environment in which you function. We take much of that environment for granted without ever questioning why certain situations exist.

As part of the DA's Pentagon stress-management program, for example, work groups were brought together to discuss their work norms and values. During one session, participants complained that on the job, they were continually stopping to answer the telephone, no matter what they were doing on any particular day. The group's manager had ruled that no phone would ring three times without being answered. The result of this policy was an externally driven prioritization system. As a result, these staff members often worked well into the night and on weekends to complete their assigned workloads, creating substantial personal as well as on-the-job stress.

Once the manager changed the orders and appointed one person to answer the phones, the others could remain focused on their assigned tasks. Efficiency and productivity increased; stress decreased. The fix was simple—however, it took an external consultant to reduce this high level of environmental stress.

In every group attending the stress-reduction seminars, an attempt was made to instill a new norm, termed a Hunza holiday: Group members were encouraged to sit quietly at their desks and close their eyes for a few minutes at a time. Previously, most participants felt they had to appear busy every moment of the day to remain in the good graces of their superiors and/or peers.

EXERCISE 1: THE HUNZA HOLIDAY

The Hunza holiday is named after the people of Hunza, Afghanistan, who are renowned for their longevity. This technique involves closing your eyes for a few minutes, relaxing, and not thinking about the task at hand.

Take a few deep cleansing breaths. Use a slow count of ten as you intake breath; and again, when you exhale, use a slow count of ten. Exhaling slowly will facilitate the release of your tensions and worries, allowing you to reach a calm state of mind quickly in most environments.

Do this now.

It is that simple to begin. The big step is *allowing yourself* to take the time to do it. How many of you read on without doing the exercise, even though it is relatively quick and simple? You will be surprised at how quickly this simple procedure gets you back on track. It is a great way to gain insight, allow access to personal intuition, and elicit a "Eureka effect" when problems become stumbling blocks because no solution is immediately obvious. The technique works best if practiced for short periods—about five minutes each—several times a day or as needed.

Once you have given yourself permission to close your eyes and relax, the next step is to choose a place where you can be undisturbed. If your immediate office is unsatisfactory, innovate. One place usually available is a bathroom stall—very few people will bother you there. Other private places may exist in your work environment; it is just a matter of finding them. A quiet place is preferable but not necessary. The more experienced you become at using these techniques, the easier it will be to focus your thoughts or attain calm regardless of the surrounding environment. Initially, do all you can to make relaxation easy: Whatever reduces sensory input (such as sight and sound) will help.

The correlation between your state of mind and your physical state is direct. In our society, as well as in most of the military, people are physically tense most of the time. Many don't even remember what it is like to relax physically, let alone mentally.

A recently retired colonel told us, "You don't have any idea how fast we've been running all these years." This colonel had just taken three months off before entering civilian life. Many people believe they thrive on setting and maintaining an incredible working pace. They get into a groove and are carried along, frequently letting external priorities drive them. Top generals have been known to lament that there was no one around them who had time to stop and really think. Executives and middle managers are frequently too busy "fighting fires" to do the in-depth thinking required to create a high-performance organization. As leaders in one government agency put it, "We don't put out fires, we just piss on the highest flames."

To gain control of the mind, we will work first on the body. For those of you who don't know what a relaxed state feels like, our second exercise is a simple procedure for attaining one.

EXERCISE 2: MUSCLE RELAXATION

First, assume a comfortable position. Lie down or sit in a chair that allows you to move about slightly and relax. We don't suggest using your bed. It's too easy to fall asleep there since the body and mind have a programmed response for that location.

Close your eyes. Listen to the sounds around you. Be aware of your body and what it is telling you. Where are you experiencing pressure? Is it from the floor or where you are sitting? Are your clothes too snug? Are you experiencing any discomfort? Feel free at this point to make adjustments. Move about until you get into the most comfortable position possible. Loosen any tight clothing. Take out your wallet if you have it in your back pocket. Loosen or slip off your shoes; if you wear glasses, take them off: Shoes and eyeglasses tell the mind-body system it's ready for business. Keep your legs and arms uncrossed as you proceed with this exercise. During relaxation procedures, the pressure of crossed limbs may be distracting. Tell yourself mentally to relax. Take a deep breath, close your eyes, and imagine that breath spreading throughout your body, from your scalp to your toes. Exhale slowly.

Now that you have gotten a feel for your body, tighten the muscles in one of your arms. Make a fist and then tense the entire arm as tightly as possible. Hold that tension for a few seconds—five or ten seconds will be long enough if you really tighten the muscle. Next, quickly release the tension. Pay attention to the sensation in your arm as the muscles relax. Concentrate on that feeling. Get to know it so that you can recognize when those muscles are relaxed.

Now repeat the process with your other arm. Do only one arm at a time. Concentrate on the *feeling* of physical relaxation. After you have experimented with each arm, repeat the process with your legs, one at a time. Again, direct your mind to focus on the *feeling* of physical relaxation. The goal of these exercises is to develop a quick recognition of the sensation of physical relaxation.

After working with each of your limbs, try manipulating several major muscle groups at the same time. Eventually, you can tense your entire body and then allow it to relax.

As with any exercise, don't overdo it. We are establishing cues that will result in long-term learning, not preparing you to pass a test in tensing your muscles. It is the mental cataloging of physical relaxation that is important. Just practice doing one or two repetitions a day for a few days, until you have physically cataloged the *expectation* of the desired effect. A benefit you may notice after just a few days of practicing this simple exercise is that you will become more aware of the sources and indications of stress in your life and will have acquired a new tool to cope better with it.

When you try this exercise, be sure that you are not in a position conducive to falling asleep. Many high-pressure executives, as well as others, have only two modes of physical functioning: either they are in "balls-to-the-wall" mode or they are fast asleep, with no available increments in between.

This on/off modality is exemplified by the plight of one of the generals being trained in stress management: To provide minimal interruption to his hectic schedule, he was given a simple biofeedback device to take home. A few days later, he returned the device, saying that it didn't work. The only thing that happened when he used it was that he fell asleep. It became apparent throughout questioning that this general actually had no incremental relaxed states available—he'd trained himself into on/off mode. If he stopped working and allowed himself to begin physically relaxing, the mind took that as a signal to shut down and he went immediately to sleep.

In a later chapter we will cover biofeedback systems and the use of the electroencephalograph (EEG) in biofeedback. Know now that when the brain waves of meditators are compared to the brain waves of people in other states of consciousness, a clear and discernible difference is noted. Meditation is not simply a relaxed state close to sleep; during meditation, a person's EEG resembles an awake state, although the body is quite relaxed. Just become aware of your own ability to physically relax.

To quiet the mind, there are two different approaches you may employ. One is a process of concentration; the other, a process of detachment. Both are good techniques. Try them both and see which works better for you.

EXERCISE 3: QUICK CALMING

The first mental technique is to repeat silently to yourself, "I am calm." This easy concentration technique diverts your mind from the immediate environment and crystallizes the physical and mental state you wish to achieve.

Try it now. Close your eyes. Take a couple of deep breaths. Repeat mentally, "I am calm," or an equivalent statement that conveys the same meaning: "I am serene"; "I'm feeling safe, warm, and secure." Do this for a minute or two.

After trying this simple exercise, take note of how you feel both physically and mentally. When using this technique, as with all exercises, be aware of the states you are producing. Your goal is to be able to attain these relaxed states at will. You are now building a road map that will allow you to find the same feelings again under conditions that may not be as conducive to relaxation. We recommend integrating this technique with the previous exercises. Doing so allows you to relax the body and mind in unison.

Our second mental exercise uses repetitious sounds or tonal vibrations that have no particular meaning but are useful in emptying the mind. One sound that is familiar to most people is *om*, or *aum*. This ancient Sanskrit word is said to replicate the basic sound of the universe. Such chants, used around the world, often have a very soothing effect. The purpose of the pure monosyllabic tonal qualities of *aum* is one of repetition, to free the mind of all thoughts via detachment, rather than to analyze complex and abstract concepts.

While the tonal approach is not recommended for use in the workplace, it is of great benefit when creating deeper states of relaxation within yourself. These states, once mastered, can also be instantly accessed with sufficient training.

EXERCISE 4: SINGLE THOUGHT CONTROL

At home or in a private place, begin by repeating the integrated physical and mental relaxation techniques previously recommended. Start with exercise one—take a few cleansing breaths. Then perform exercise two and relax your body. Once you are physically relaxed, perform exercise three. (After you are familiar with these techniques, exercises two and three can be integrated into a single step.)

When you are sufficiently calm, intone, slowly and loudly, the sounds or words you have chosen. Do this five times. Repeat the process, intoning more quickly and less loudly. Continue until nothing is discernible but the movement of the lips. Do this for twenty to thirty minutes or until you have finished the process. We recommend choosing tones or words with inherent rhythm; they should flow like music yet have sufficient key syllables to aid your concentration. Concentrating helps exclude unwanted thoughts. We also recommend that the beginner choose sounds or word-trains of medium length to achieve a rhythmic flow. *Aum*, or *om*, while popular with advanced students, is too short to be sufficiently rhythmical and is not recommended for use by the novice, who might choose to repeat *I am calm* instead. As you practice any of the described techniques, external thoughts may intrude. This is quite common, even for advanced meditators. One solution is to gently acknowledge the thought and then return to your word or sound.

Do not become distracted by focusing on the intruding thought; you may then find it more difficult to banish the thought from your mind. For this reason, we suggest acknowledging the thought before returning to the exercise. Often, the intruding thought is an answer to a problem you have been unable to solve. By acknowledging that you have received the information and will work on it later, your subconscious mind should stop intruding and allow you to return to the activity.

Remember, ultimately your purpose is to control your mind, to be able to think *one chosen thought*, without interruption, for as long as you desire.

The next exercise in our arsenal of mental techniques for quieting the mind is meditation. Stilling the conscious mind is the ultimate idea of meditation, a preliminary step toward focusing mental powers on a single point. Many members of the military practice meditation; it has never been adopted as a training technique, although several proposals to do this have been put forward.

EXERCISE 5: SPOT MEDITATION

We will now learn to use any handy object as a concentration aid. This meditative form of concentration to quiet the mind can be as simple as picking an object to focus on and then observing what happens.

Try this easy technique immediately. First relax, using the methods you learned in the previous exercises. Now pick a spot on the wall that you can see easily. Don't strain by turning your neck or stretching to see the spot. Now focus all your attention on the spot. Start noticing things about the spot. What is its color? Shape? Texture? How big is it? What made it? How did it get there? As you watch the spot, are you able to stay focused on it?

After a short time, many will notice their thoughts beginning to wander. Acknowledge them and let them go. As an observer of yourself, how long did it take for you to realize that your thoughts had wandered? Was it your last work effort that found its way back in? Try to keep count of how many times your thoughts wander. Do this for as long as you can.

Initially, your thoughts may wander after only a minute or two. Total concentration can be fatiguing. The *effort* of focusing on the object of concentration is most important. Twenty-minute to half-hour intervals give plenty of time for a novice to practice this technique.

Frequently, while meditating on a point, you will find solutions to problems previously unresolvable. In time, the number of breaks in your concentration will decrease. However, as you begin to make progress, there usually is a period when they become more frequent. Do not be concerned. This is caused by an increase in your powers of observation. With time, your control will improve.

Using a spot on the wall has many advantages in an office setting. Spots are usually present and few people will notice you looking at them. In fact, they probably won't know what you are looking at, or even care much, unless you make this a major part of your day. Any object can be used as your focal point. The key to this exercise is in establishing an environment in which practice will be safe and acceptable.

Traditional focus-objects for improving concentration include both the flower and the candle. The flower allows multiple observations: colors, textures, sizes, smells, shapes, and subcomponents. The flame is another classical concentration aid, primarily because fire holds an enduring fascination for most people. Sitting around a fireplace or a campfire, it seems easy to let yourself become lost in thought. A candle is an ideal concentration aid. If you practice with a flame, remember to pick a safe place for the candle. Be sure that the location is free of drafts so that the flame remains relatively constant.

In all these exercises, be aware of the changes occurring within you. Observe all aspects of yourself, including your physiology, your breathing, and what is taking place inside your mind. Remember, you are learning to attain and maintain these states as *effortlessly* as possible. Once the structured habit-pattern is there, you will be able to expand your mental and intuitive capabilities. But this supporting structure must be architecturally sound and firmly established.

Concentration is a very valuable tool. Exceptional managers use this technique when conducting business. Top-level executives frequently must handle diverse and complex problems with extremely short transition periods. In the Pentagon, generals move from one meeting to another or have back-to-back briefings on topics that may range from acquisition of new high-technology weapons systems, to personnel issues, to adjusting multimillion-dollar funding priorities, to addressing base closure problems that are politically sensitive. The briefers may be lined up, going in one after another, each thinking that his or her issue is the hottest thing on the agenda today.

To be effective, top managers must focus attention on the problem at hand. To be able to accomplish this feat takes training—the same type of training required to control and calm the mind.

Individual warriors must also be able to focus attention on the task at hand. As we will discuss in the chapter on martial arts, the fighter must discern which opposing force possesses the most danger and deal with that threat first. To accomplish this, one focuses on that threat quickly and intently, and then shifts focus to other potential attackers in a split second, before returning to the primary threat. Being ever vigilant is the key. It is a learnable skill.

Combat can serve to sharpen these skills. As a Special Forces A-Team commander in Vietnam, John Alexander quickly learned to monitor the radio even while sound asleep. The camp was Ba Xaoi, an isolated spot on the Cambodian border in the Mekong Delta. Danger was ever present, yet a person had to rest. Alexander would meditate, focusing on relaxation. When the call sign of his unit came over the radio, he could answer it as if he were waiting on the call. Frequently, hours passed between calls, which could come at any time. The ability to change focus quickly and effectively respond saved lives in the field.

No matter where you are situated in your organization, as a manager you will be required to focus intently on issues and then change focus quickly. Such switching can be demanded when you answer the phone while talking to someone else. Good managers and executives can focus attention; others don't last or are not promoted.

Once acquainted with these concentration techniques, another tool you can use to quiet the mind is advanced control of your breathing. Advanced breathing techniques are a prerequisite for advanced control of the body, as well as the mind. Breathing is something Westerners generally take for granted and only consciously consider when reaching extremes, such as running too hard or experiencing physical or psychological stress. Very few ever take the time, when in relatively relaxed states, to notice how they are breathing.

One of the best ways to control breathing, once the techniques are mastered, is by use of the intonation exercises described in exercise four.

Try this simple step: Just take a deep breath and slowly let it out. Repeat the process several times. For the first few breaths, notice consciously what it feels like to breathe. Then note the effects that deep breathing has upon your physiology. Watch how your mental state changes as you change your breathing pattern.

Many of you may already know something about simple deep breathing. The trick is to be willing and able to apply the techniques when you really need them—to be able to call them up when under mounting stress, fully confident that they will work for you. Many executives get caught up in the immediate problem, not realizing who or what is in control. With practice, preferably on a regular basis, these techniques will become second nature and readily employable.

Most people think of breathing as a two-stage process—

inhaling and exhaling. Breathing as a two-stage process is best practiced by using a direct inhale-to-exhale ratio of one to four. This can be accomplished comfortably by inhaling for a count of four and exhaling for a count of sixteen. In cultures with a tradition of meditation, there are considered to be four stages of breathing. In addition to inhaling and exhaling, two pauses are added. These pauses are quite important.

The four-part cycle of breathing is: exhale; hold empty; inhale; and hold full. Do not force the cycle when you first start. Beware of hyperventilating at first. Most of us are not accustomed to exhaling, then holding our breath, even for a very few seconds. Breathe through your nose initially. More advanced techniques require you to inhale through your nose and slowly exhale through your mouth.

EXERCISE 6: CONTROLLED BREATHING
Exercise six is a three-part breathing exercise using a direct ratio of one to four to two. It should be done as follows:

- inhale for a count of four;
- hold for a count of sixteen;
- exhale slowly for a count of eight.

As you become more proficient, maintain the relative ratios of inhalation/exhalation. Do not just extend the phase that is easiest for you. For best results, you should practice twice a day for fifteen to twenty minutes at a time.

There appears to be a cumulative effect to meditating. If done consistently for a period of time, you will notice personal benefits that should increase your desire to pursue further applications. These benefits may include, but are not limited to, being more relaxed, being able to handle stress better, clarity of thought, and a reduced requirement for sleep.

The idea that meditation can be helpful is based on far more than subjective reporting by practitioners. Many scientific studies have been conducted on the physiological effects of meditating. Significantly beneficial results have been published in many journals.[1]

Many of these studies were done in the 1970s, some under grants provided by the National Institute of Mental Health. Most indicated that meditation induces beneficial physiological changes, including reduced heart rate, lowered oxygen consumption, and lowered blood pressure.[2]

Today, a major cause of death, especially among males, is hypertension. A dramatic relationship between stress and cancer has also been demonstrated.[3] Stress kills.

The Western executive is more highly stressed than counterparts in rigidly controlled societies. Studies comparing the relative stress on citizens of open societies to those in hierarchal societies found that the incidence of heart disease was significantly greater in citizens of open societies. Members of controlled societies who immigrated to more open societies demonstrated a correlative increase in heart disease, attributable to new psychosocial stresses.[4]

Stress can cause us to lose perspective—and with it, control. There are times when life seems totally out of control. The precipitating factor may be a true tragedy, such as the death or serious injury of a loved one, or a perceived crisis, such as blowing an exam or being late for a date. Each individual has a different tolerance threshold for crisis. In today's workplace, crisis management has become a norm rather than an exception. The successful manager is the one best qualified to simultaneously handle stress and draw order from chaos.

The military has long been aware that how you train is how you will fight. Combat is an extremely stressful experience. When first confronted with a combat situation, a warrior does not have the luxury of attempting various strategies. If unsuccessful on the first attempt, the warrior may well be dead. Therefore, combat actions and reactions are rehearsed over and over again until they become automatic. They are life savers.

The following crisis-management tools may also be life savers, emotionally and even physically. During periods of great depression and despair, people resort to desperate acts. By having preset strategies, you'll be able to recoup more quickly, manage the immediate crisis, and regain equilibrium.

The first step is to gain control. The act may be as simple as picking up a pencil or calling someone on the phone. You may want to express how you feel or outline what you want to do. Despair frequently comes from feeling helpless to control events. For most of us, there is nothing worse than helplessness in the face of our present situation or, even worse, our own destiny.

By analyzing the problem on paper or by talking to someone about it, we can confront it and view it from another perspective.

Make a physical change. Stand up. Go for a walk. Take a brief vacation. Get some distance between you and the stressor—psychologically and, if possible, physically. Realize that the problem will seem different, and often less overwhelming, from a new vantage point. If you can, get other opinions on the situation. Panic often locks us into a myopic view of a situation. This tunnel vision can prove extremely unhealthy. Remember, there *is* an appropriate time and place to cry or scream. This natural reaction can prevent serious health and psychological problems in the long run. The legacy of "Big boys and big girls don't cry" is one of exacerbated stress, counterproductive to good mental health.

During a period when you consider yourself to be whole and in charge, take inventory of your life. Make lists that include:

- personal relationships—who supports you and how
- accomplishments—what you have done that you are proud of
- assets—financial and others
- skills—an inventory of what you can do well

Keep these lists where you can find them. Review them from time to time. In a crisis, they may be invaluable in providing a pathway to perspective and renewed hope. This is one example of being prepared to deal with a subsequent crisis.

An immediate meditation drill for crisis situations is our last exercise for this chapter. If you have reached a critical point of anger or frustration, this will help calm you.

EXERCISE 7: INSTANT RELAX

Sitting or standing, take a single breath. Hold it. Align fingers and palms as if you were about to pray. Press your thumbs against the center of your chest, approximately over the solar plexus, and lower your chin to touch the tips of your middle fingers. Still holding your breath, push your hands together isometrically, five times in succession. Now slowly exhale.

If you are excited or upset, this exercise will help you rapidly, sometimes nearly instantaneously, achieve a physically calm state. Once your physical excitation is under control, you can think more clearly.

As Confucius said, "he who conquers himself is the mightiest warrior." The warrior must be able to control the mind under any conditions. The warrior moves from a relaxed state to instant action, totally focused on the task or threat at hand. The warrior never wastes energy. Once the threat is vanquished, the obstacle overcome, the warrior returns to a calm mental state.

The *I Ching* warns: "If you are agitated in mind, and your thoughts go hither and thither, only those friends on whom you fix your conscious thoughts will follow." As we embark, in the next chapter, on the path of influence, a quiet mind will be your greatest asset.

3

INFLUENCE: THE ART AND SCIENCE OF INFLUENCE TECHNOLOGY

The warrior must be able to *consciously* influence others.

Just as politics is a controlled attempt to influence a domestic constituency, diplomacy is a measured attempt to exert national will upon another nation or group of nations. When an attempt at international influence breaks down and global imperatives are not met, warfare often results.

Warfare may be the ultimate influence technology. Warfare as influence, however, has a serious drawback: it is based upon chaos; control degenerates as war fighting continues. The warrior must be ever vigilant, always prepared for combat, while using all his skills to avoid the opening of hostilities. Preserving the peace is the conscious, ultimate aim of the true warrior.

The abilities to be decisive, to guide others, and to build cohesive fighting units are prerequisites of the military leader and necessary components of the warrior spirit. To lead effectively, you must clearly and concisely articulate your objective to others and then influence them to help secure that objective. This holds true not only in senior/subordinate relationships but in all relationships.

Influence: The Art and Science of Influence Technology

We influence others continually. Most people do so unconsciously, in an uncontrolled way. Too many haven't the vaguest idea of the outcome they desire or how to secure assistance in attaining their goals. Power lies in consciously influencing others.

To begin on the path of influence, you must envision where you wish to go or what you need to accomplish. You then develop a plan, sketch a rational road map for its execution, and see it through to fruition.

Most of us are aware that we're subjected to the art of influence every day. Whether by the news media, Madison Avenue, domestic politicians, or international propagandists, the effects of these influences are visible, if not always clear. Hidden agendas, subterfuges, and ploys are part of the art. Influence technology is a serious and potentially deadly game.

The Soviets, past masters of propaganda and disinformation, have been researching methods of influencing human behavior for over sixty years. They have extensively explored an influence technology we call controlled offensive behavior, defined as "research on human vulnerability as it applies to methods of influencing or altering human behavior."[1]

A declassified Defense Intelligence Agency (DIA) report, *Controlled Offensive Behavior—USSR* that evaluated Soviet research in this area was "intended as an aid in the development of countermeasures for the protection of U.S. or allied personnel."[2] Some of the revolutionary techniques studied by the Soviets to influence human behavior include: "biochemicals, sound, light, color, odors, sensory deprivation, sleep, electronic and magnetic fields, hypnosis, autosuggestion, and paranormal phenomena (psychokinesis, extrasensory perception, astral projection, dream state, clairvoyance, and precognition)."[3]

DIA estimates of the strategic threat posed by Soviet psi research postulate that sooner or later they will be able to:

"a) Know the contents of top secret U.S. documents, the movements of our troops and ships and the location and nature of our military installations.

b) Mold the thoughts of key U.S. military and civilian leaders, at a distance.

c) Cause the instant death of any U.S. official, at a distance.

d) Disable, at a distance, U.S. military equipment of all types including spacecraft."[4]

This gives us a disturbing view of the future, even in view of perestroika, glasnost, and Soviet internal problems. We can only hope that the Soviets offer to share this research with us in a spirit of new openness.

An unclassified 1976 study commissioned by CIA confirms that "the Soviets are investigating the psychophysiology of multimodel, programmed stimulation as a method to entrain physiological rhythms and produce changes in states of consciousness."[5]

Some high-end influence technologies may already have been employed against us. According to Robert C. Beck, director of the Bio-Medical Research Associates of Los Angeles, the Soviets have been utilizing extreme low frequency (ELF) radio waves (frequencies under 3 kilohertz [KHz] are considered ELF; ELF frequencies under 20 Hertz [Hz] are below the range of human hearing and are termed infrasound) modulated at pulse repetition rates of five to fifteen Hz at amplitudes of up to 40 megawatts. Although the source of these signals is believed to be an Over-the-Horizon RADAR (OTHR), the RADAR in question may have a dual purpose. According to Dr. Beck, "These frequencies fall precisely within the psychoactive range of neuronal synchronization or brainwave entrainment, where subjects experience states from increased anxiety to extreme disorientation and even unconsciousness."[6]

The type of disorientation associated with these signals was reported in the U.S. as far back as the mid-1970s, when West Coast residents, notably from Eugene, Oregon, "complained about odd atmospheric sensations causing headaches, dry throats, depression, high anxiety, irritability and loss of sleep."[7] Extremely specialized equipment is required to measure and confirm the presence of such signals. If potentially detrimental experimentation is being performed on an unaware test population of Americans, its presence needs to be officially confirmed.

We explain the techniques of influence technology for two purposes:

1. To give you the tools to recognize whether influence technology is being employed against you, and to neutralize its effects.

2. To teach you to use its more benign capabilities, on a personal and professional level, to influence others.

NEW PATTERNS OF INFLUENCE

Neuro-linguistic programming (NLP) is defined as a set of techniques used to facilitate individual pattern changes.[8] Techniques found useful by many senior U.S. Army officers are based on this trademarked program. NLP teaches ways to modify behavior patterns that are not useful as well as to install useful behavior patterns.

NLP, formulated by Richard Bandler (a mathematician and computer expert) and John Grinder (a linguist), was introduced to the U.S. Army via a program called New Patterns of Influence. In addition to the NLP basics, this program contained information from the U.S. Army's Organizational Effectiveness School (dissolved in 1984 due to budget constraints), as well as original thinking by Lieutenant Colonel Frank Burns and Bob Klaus on skills required for military leadership.

This course, carefully packaged as a three-day intensive, was presented to selected general officers and Senior Executive Service (SES) members. Among the first generals to take the course was then-Lieutenant General Maxwell Thurman, who later went on to receive his fourth star and become Vice-Chief of Staff of the Army (VCSA) and Commander, U.S. Southern Command. General Thurman, who distinguished himself as SOUTHCOM's leader during the Dec. 20, 1989 U.S. invasion of Panama, is well known as bright, forward thinking, and innovative.

It was General Thurman's support that allowed the NLP training group to make inroads with many other generals. In fact, he commissioned a study of human performance by the National Academy of Science, monitored by the Army Research Institute. General Thurman has kept interest alive through his personal influence.

This program was considered effective by a great majority of the several hundred who attended over a period of four years. In 1983, the NLP training group, along with John Alexander, was engaged to teach these skills to several members of Congress, including Al Gore, Jr. and Tom Downey, under the auspices of Congressional Clearing House on the Future, a bipartisan activity established to provide information to congressmen when they request it. Gore went on to become a serious candidate in the 1988 presidential primary race.

Other skill-enhancing courses were provided to various military organizations. One organization that played a major role in the dissemination of NLP skills was the U.S. Army Intelligence and Security Command (INSCOM). During the early 1980s, INSCOM was commanded by Major General Albert N. Stubblebine. Like Thurman, Stubblebine was a visionary in the realm of creativity. Unlike the rest of the U.S. Army, INSCOM does not differentiate between wartime and peacetime roles. The soldiers assigned there actively engage in intelligence-gathering and counterintelligence missions on a daily basis. Stubblebine continually searched for the best available techniques to provide the warrior's edge to troops engaged in this often dangerous business. After attending an early session, Stubblebine became an active supporter of NLP, employing the techniques personally and throughout the command.

Under the auspices of Major General Stubblebine, several advanced human technologies were extensively explored by the military. Unfortunately, there was a price to pay for venturing too far beyond the bunkers of conventional wisdom: Stubblebine retired from the service prematurely, after running headlong into the marshalled forces of the status quo.

This lesson should not go unnoticed. When you choose to

apply the lessons learned in this book, be sure you constantly perform environmental checks. It is in your own best interest to be aware of how much stress you place on those around you, especially superiors. Keep in mind *their* belief systems, and how they might accept your practices. We are not suggesting limits on your practice and application of skills, just judicious caution in how open you are with others.

LEADERSHIP AND INFLUENCE

The warrior may apply influence in a number of ways over individuals or groups. When this influence is applied to friendly or even ambivalent individuals, it is called leadership—the art of getting others to do what you want them to do, when you want it done and to the standards you set. Like any other subject, leadership can be taught, and most people have differing amounts of innate ability. What we will provide are some of the basic tools for improving your abilities in this area, regardless of your entry-level skills.

There are three main rules of effective influence:

1. know your desired outcome—precisely;
2. be flexible in your behavior—keep an open mind;
3. be observant enough to know when your outcome has been achieved.

While these rules may sound simple, it takes concentration and practice to apply them. The rules hold for influencing both groups and individuals.

Know your desired outcome: Many people wander through life haphazardly, having events thrust upon them, not understanding or realizing how these events occur or what generates them. They approach life reactively rather than proactively. When stating a desire, they use generalities such as "I want people to like me better." Being "liked" is nonspecific. It affords no clear way to measure if, when, or to what degree we have become "liked."

Outcomes should be specific and *stated in a positive way*. This is important, because we often move *toward* our dominant thought. If we state goals negatively, we may unintentionally energize the opposite of our intended outcome. How many times have you been told, "Whatever you do, don't . . ." and then gone on to do exactly what you were told not to? This is an example of being pulled toward your dominant thought.

An example of a desire—and desirable—outcome might be securing a superior's approval for a project of yours.

To achieve that goal, state it in detail. Include project approval by the individual, at a certain time, with the appropriate resources. Each qualifier should be spelled out. Anyone who has prepared a project proposal knows that resourcing is a key issue. Often, projects are approved with insufficient money or personnel to assure a satisfactory degree of completion. Taking it (the resources) out of hide can be a worse outcome than no approval at all. Having to accomplish more with less is a common trap that can be avoided.

Before attempting influence intervention, it is best to scout the terrain. This means learning as much as possible about the situation *before* determining your outcome or attempting to sway an individual or group. The situation will vary from case to case. Sometimes you will know a lot about the group or individual you wish to influence; at other times you will go in relatively cold. When you go in cold, you must assess the audience quickly and precisely, and immediately begin establishing control.

What impressed the general officers most about influence technologies was the ability to capture an individual's attention without betraying the amount of influence exerted. The first influence technique is used to gain rapport with those you wish to influence.

EXERCISE 1: BODY MIRRORING
People are most comfortable with those similar to themselves. You've probably gone to a party or a new school where you didn't know anyone. What was the first thing you did? Most

people will begin looking for others with common experiences, to whom they can relate.

Certain people seem to gain rapport with others quite easily; some don't. This technique consciously allows you to gain rapport with anyone you wish to influence. By reversing the technique, you can distance yourself from anyone you choose.

First, observe the person you want to influence. This can be done quickly, even in a chance meeting. Using visual input as well as auditory cues, your objective is to become similar to that person in posture and language.

Unobtrusively, assume the same body position as the target. Become a mirror of the other person. Align your body with his or hers. Place your hands in the same position as his or hers, and then your legs. Watch the tilt of the head and mirror that as well. Assume this position slowly—do not be obvious while you are mirroring.

If the person is in an exaggerated position, approximate a less extreme position. If the person is standing on his or her head, for example, wait until he or she is finished before attempting to mirror. Be subtle in your movements. Very few people become consciously aware of mirroring. They feel attracted to you for some reason they can't quite explain.

Once you have mirrored someone, begin following movements. Again, be subtle as you mirror the moves. Do not be obvious to the other person—this is not a game of Simon Says, where children mimic each other quite openly. A short time delay in shifting positions will help mask your activity.

To practice this technique, you might start with a friend who is aware of the process, and take turns. Once you are comfortable mirroring that person, try it on other friends without prior discussion. Again, be subtle. Mirror for a few minutes at a time. There is no hurry. You'll find numerous opportunities to practice on anyone you meet. In a short time, mirroring will become second nature and you'll be able to ease into it automatically without betraying your intent to others.

Remember that the objective of mirroring is to influence others on demand. Once this technique is mastered, be sure you are sending the message you *want* others to receive. You have opened a transmitter and you are broadcasting. Do it consciously and with the purpose of everyone gaining from such interaction.

We must caution you to influence with integrity. There is truth in the old saying "What goes around, comes around." We urge you to practice the art of influence with the best interest of all parties in mind. The warrior exerts his influence in keeping with a code of honor and an unassailable integrity above reproach. With these tools comes the responsibility for right action. Our purpose in providing you with advanced human technology techniques is to help enhance *all* human performance. Properly used, these techniques can have a positive impact on human interaction worldwide.

EXERCISE 2: BREATHING LOCK

Once you are a master of physical mirroring, you may wish to match breathing with your target of influence. Although very subtle, this is a powerful technique. Under its influence, the other person will be quite susceptible to what you say. The objective is to align your breathing pattern with the target's, as closely as possible.

This technique takes both practice and close observation. Some people are heavy breathers; their pattern will be obvious to you. Others are shallow. If a shallow breather is heavily clothed, you must learn where and how to look to discern his or her pattern.

If the stomach is exposed to view, start there. Otherwise, a telltale area usually in view is the area around the shoulders. Carefully watch for a rise and fall of one or both shoulders. This may take some practice. Practice whenever you are in the company of others. With experience, you'll be able to ascertain the breathing pattern quickly and easily synchronize your own.

As with mirroring, don't be too obvious. If your target has just finished a sporting event and is gasping for breath, wait until a normal breathing pattern is resumed before attempting to match it.

If the person has a breathing pattern greatly different from yours, you may find it difficult to actually match that pattern. Don't end up gasping for air while trying to emulate someone who breathes much more slowly than you. The best technique for such a situation is to keep track of the target's pattern with another part of your body. For example, use one of your fingers, or a foot movement, to keep time with the breathing. Do this within his or her peripheral vision, without being too obvious.

Once learned, this powerful tool provides rapport with another person at a level below the target's conscious awareness.

EXERCISE 3: SIMPLE SHIFT

Now that you have gained rapport with your target of influence, the next step is to test the strength of that rapport. Slowly change to a position different from the target's current one. A target who has slipped into rapport with you will follow your lead unconsciously.

Start simply, by crossing your legs or moving an arm. If rapport has been firmly established, the target will mirror you. This is known as a simple shift. If you don't get the desired response initially, resume mirroring. Then go back and once again test the rapport.

When first trying these techniques, you will probably be surprised at their effectiveness. Practice on a daily basis, and your capabilities will expand rapidly. Soon you will have a broad range of influence tools at your command.

Once having achieved rapport and successfully led your subject through a simple shift, expand the change you wish to induce. Make your movements a bit bolder. Test the limits of your ability to influence the other person. Again, remember that integrity is essential in this process: act in the best interest of both parties. A "win-win" strategy supports influence technologies, because unconscious cues you display will indicate your enthusiasm and sincerity.

So far, we have dealt exclusively with the body-language aspects of rapport. Another key element is auditory. Choice of language reveals how people think and what is important to them. Learn to listen actively to what people say. They will provide you with clues to their values and beliefs. In conversation, one who merely awaits his turn to talk misses valuable information offered—consciously and unconsciously—by fellows and risks showing insincerity with a vacant-eyed stare. *Everyone* wants to be listened to, and understood. All parties benefit if you are an attentive and sophisticated listener.

People will often *tell* you how to influence them if you let them.

INFORMATION PROCESSING

Research suggests that behavior is determined by an organism's internal flow of information.[9] Although this flow cannot be seen, it logically must involve functions such as "attention, receiving information through the sensory mechanisms, perception, coding and decoding, learning, memory, recall, reasoning, making judgments, making decisions, transmitting information, and executing physical responses."[10]

In the following model, the binary digit, or bit, is the unit of measurement for information. The estimated maximum flow of information in the process of sensory reception is 1 billion bits per second. Yet the maximum flow of information into the neural connections is only 3 million bits per second.[11] A process of intermediate reduction leads to a conscious perception of the various incoming stimuli. This model is based loosely on the Broadbent[12] conception of information flow within a nervous system:

Information flow is a process of coding and decoding. Influence technologies allow you to get deeper inside the loop, thus increasing your odds for entering the limited-capacity channel, where you can make a lasting impression. In this model, the

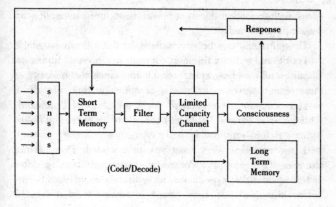

nervous system is portrayed as a single channel with a limited capacity for information transmission. The key here is the filter.

In signal-communication theory, ambient or environmental noise or interference is always present that may garble or in other ways detract from transmitted signals before they arrive at their intended reception point.[13] Filters help diminish the effects of such noise and ensure the integrity of the signal. If the noise is too great, the intended signals may not reach their destination. Influence technology helps distinguish the intended signals from the noise and helps minimize the actual noise levels themselves.

Sensory information is acquired in two main ways: visually (by sight); and auditorially (by sound). Information is also processed kinesthetically (by touch) and olfactorally (by smell).

Everyone has a preferred mode for absorbing information. Most people have a dominant mode (visual) supported by the other modes of operation. A few people work primarily in only one domain. Be aware of the difference; you can use it to your distinct advantage by distinguishing the thinking patterns of others and adjusting the way you present information to them accordingly.

When choosing between the visual and auditory mode to

transmit information during a presentation, certain criteria are generally accepted.

These criteria can be summarized by the following table:[14]

Traditional military briefings concentrate on visual input, including slides, viewgraphs, and charts, since the majority of Americans operate visually. An exception to this rule was a former commanding general of the Army Materiel Command. This four-star general would sit back, close his eyes, and *listen*. Many briefers erroneously believed he was sleeping through their presentations, or at least was uninterested. This was not the case: This general processed information auditorially. After listening carefully, eyes closed, he invariably made cogent comments and good decisions—much to the relief of distressed briefers.

Once the general's information-processing style was understood, a few adept briefers changed format when facing him. They would come in, sit down at his desk, and talk him through the logic of their arguments. These understanding few enjoyed a high success rate because they were operating in the general's comfort zone, rather than forcing him to translate from their format to his own internal system.

Information accessing occurs in a series of steps. Short-

Use auditory presentation if:	Use visual presentation if:
1. the message is simple.	1. the message is complex.
2. the message is short.	2. the message is long.
3. the message will not be referred to later.	3. the message will be referred to later.
4. the message deals with events in time.	4. the message deals with location in space.
5. the message calls for immediate action.	5. the message does not call for immediate action.
6. the visual system of the person is overburdened.	6. the auditory system of the person is overburdened.
7. the receiving location is too bright or dark-adoption integrity is necessary.	7. the receiving location is too noisy.
8. the person's job requires him to move about continually.	8. the person's job allows him to remain in one position.

cutting this process puts you more closely in touch with your intended audience, providing an edge.

EXERCISE 4: COMFORT ZONING

Now we will learn to distinguish representational systems by listening when others talk. In this exercise, you must listen actively. When you do, you will hear your target unconsciously *describe for you* his or her preferred intake modality or representational system. You need only ask questions designed to elicit a response demonstrating the target's grasp of some concept. The way he or she describes their orientation to the concept will key you to the target's preferred intake modality.

Visually oriented people use words predominantly dealing with vision: They say things like, "I get the picture," or, "I see what you mean," or, "That's clear to me."

Aurally oriented people say things like, "I hear what you're saying," or, "I like the sound of that," or, "Let's talk about this."

The relative few who function best kinesthetically will tell you: "I can get in touch with that," or, "I grasp the situation," or, "I have a firm handle on it."

Most people do use *all* of the representational systems to some degree. You are listening for the target's *dominant* system. The target is telling you how he or she prefers to input information and process it. You must be flexible enough to switch your method of presenting information to him or her. By getting as far into the preferred system, or comfort zone, as possible, you minimize the amount of internal translation the target must do. Every time an item of information must be translated or reinterpreted, there is a probability that it will be distorted. By presenting information simply, in the preferred mode of the recipient, you reduce the chances for distortion of your message, increasing your ability to get your message across and your chances of success.

You can learn how others think by watching their eye-movement patterns. Bandler and Grinder (the creators of NLP) popularized this approach, which suggests that the direction of eye movement reveals whether a person is processing information in a visual, auditory or kinesthetic mode.

The most common eye accessing patterns are illustrated in figure 2. When the eyes go up, people operate in a visual mode internally: They "see" pictures in the mind's eye. Most people, when looking up and leftward, are recalling images seen previously. When the eyes go up and rightward, people are usually constructing images of what something *might* look like rather than recalling something previously seen.

When eyes move sideward, people are usually operating in an auditory mode. As before, if eyes go left, people are recalling sounds or words heard previously. If eyes move to the right, people are probably constructing words or sounds they have not heard before, such as formulating an answer to a new question.

When eyes go down, the meaning is a bit more complex. A movement down and to the left is called auditory digital. This movement indicates that the mind is carrying on an internal dialogue, running through how the response will sound and

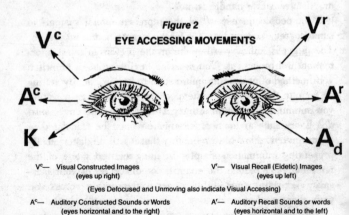

Figure 2
EYE ACCESSING MOVEMENTS

Vᶜ — Visual Constructed Images
(eyes up right)

Vʳ — Visual Recall (Eidetic) Images
(eyes up left)

(Eyes Defocused and Unmoving also indicate Visual Accessing)

Aᶜ — Auditory Constructed Sounds or Words
(eyes horizontal and to the right)

Aʳ — Auditory Recall Sounds or words
(eyes horizontal and to the left)

K — Kinesthetic Feelings (also Smell, Taste)
(eyes down right)

A — Auditory Sounds or Words
(eyes down left)

checking for possible alternatives. If the eye pattern is down and to the right, they are probably experiencing a kinesthetic or feeling response.

On occasion, someone will display a blank stare called the thousand-mile stare. When this happens, the individual is usually operating visually.

A small but significant number of people reverse the pattern from right to left. Check this out when talking to each person, by asking simple questions that will elicit each basic response in turn.

EXERCISE 5: EYE CUES

For this exercise, first learn to observe eye movements. Practice initially with a cooperative person who will talk about various topics while you note how the eyes move about, and ask questions. Remember, your task is to observe, not to be thinking of the next question.

Here are some sample questions that direct your subject to the desired mode:

- What color was your bedroom when you were in high school?
- If you could create your favorite painting, what would it look like?
- Do you remember what was said at the dinner table last night?
- What would you say to a group about this problem?
- How do you feel about abortion?

Use simple, straightforward questions when you are practicing, to ensure you don't elicit complex responses. Use the same technique, after you have become proficient, to scrutinize people you wish to influence. If, after listening to them and watching their eye movements, you are still not sure of their pattern, interject a question designed to get a specific response. One or two questions should be sufficient to confirm the accessing pattern.

During the congressmen's training, whenever sensitive questions were asked, they invariably responded slowly, and went into an extensive auditory digital pattern. When asked to describe what they were doing internally, the congressmen confirmed that an internal dialogue was taking place. Due to their constant media exposure, they habitually ran questions and possible responses through their minds before they voiced their answers.

A Central Intelligence Agency trainer who was helping his son with spelling suggested that his son look up and to the left when attempting to spell a word of which he was unsure. By using this memory-recall technique, his son improved his grades. The technique can be readily applied to any subject that requires one to recall visual images such as patterns or written words. By looking up and to the left, you are literally driving the brain to the correct mode to retrieve visual data.

We have discussed how to spot a single movement, how to check and how to determine a person's operating mode. Obviously, the world is more complex than single movements. Yet people do have routine patterns used for problem solving; understanding these can help you influence them.

To influence a target successfully, you must determine how that person makes decisions. In conversation, carefully craft questions that allow you to watch the person make decisions. A sample question might be: Why did you buy the car you have now? As the answer is explained, watch closely; in particular, watch the *sequence* of the response. The sequence of responses is critical to determining how someone reasons.

A sample response might be: "I liked the way it looked" (visual); "It felt good and rode smoothly" (kinesthetic); or "The cost was right, which made sense" (auditory digital). To structure a hypothetical presentation to get a favorable response from this person, proceed as follows:

1. present pictures of the project you want approved;
2. make sure he feels comfortable about the project; and
3. provide a bottom-line figure, *in that order*.

Now you have presented your case in the order in which your target audience makes decisions. You have reduced the amount of internal translation required; by your having entered the target's comfort zone, your probability of success has increased dramatically.

If you are required to present multiple options for decision making, you can further refine this process. To increase the chance of your preference being approved, deliberately mismatch the presentation pattern of the other choices with the preferred decision pattern of the target. By doing this, you are presenting only your preferred option compatibly with the decision maker's pattern.

No amount of influence will overcome flawed logic. Be sure you have done your homework and are presenting the best option or options. Be ethical. If you find yourself presenting unethical options, it is time to do some soul-searching about the position you're in and why you are in it. When a solution proposed for briefing to the Army Policy Council was found cost-effective but detrimental to some service members, General Thurman put it best: "Some things you do because they are right, not because they are cheapest."

Let's assume you are now familiar with these skills; you need to know what to do with the information you can gather. Earlier, we discussed developing physical rapport. Now we'll apply the same techniques to language. Linguistic mirroring is the act of feeding back to the target of influence the target's own words. It is a powerful tool for gaining rapport with an individual.

We all know people who get so involved in talking that they forget to listen to others. When you come across as someone who actually hears what's being said, most people react positively. They may be consciously unaware of why they like you, but an attentive listener makes people comfortable and thus amenable to positive influence. The feedback process does not necessitate agreeing with the individual, although that may be the impression given. Feeding back can place you in a much better position—not only to disagree, but to get the target to change his or her views on a given subject.

In presentation, as well as in conversation, another effective influence tool is knowing when to keep quiet. The listener needs a chance to process the information you have provided. Too often speakers will rattle on, because they are insecure or uncomfortable with conversational lulls. Lulls can be very useful, especially when they allow the recipient of information to digest the communication and check the logic. A lull also shows the listener that you have confidence in the material presented and in yourself. By careful visual and auditory observation, you can present desired outcomes in highly persuasive terms.

ANCHORING

Once an initial rapport with an individual has been established, you can quickly regain that same state of rapport later. This reinstatement technique is known as anchoring. Anchoring is based on the neurophysiological assumption that patterns of behavior can be installed, then reactivated whenever a similar situation is encountered or created. Our unconscious installs anchors in us naturally. Remember the smells of your mother's kitchen? The sense of smell can be one of the strongest anchors. Olfactory cues make perfume sales lucrative worldwide.

Nature creates physical anchors, too. A certain kind of touch may evoke memories of pleasurable or painful events. Knowing this, you can intentionally install anchors to return your target to specific emotional states. The first step is create the desired emotional state in the individual. Although you can do this with any state, the greater the intensity of the emotion, the more solid the anchor. Having created the state, install the anchor by touching the person in a specific way. The spot you choose should be both accessible and socially acceptable. A tap on the hand, or a squeeze of the arm—a discreet touch to any physical point will do.

If you install an anchor when a person is feeling good, you can readily evoke this feeling later by touching the person in the same spot, the same way. Create the state, set the anchor, and you can use it repeatedly.

Major General Stubblebine is a very tall man with large hands who is renowned for a firm handshake. When things go very well, he adds a firm grip on the elbow to the handshake—a conscious action on his part, designed as a motivational tool to make people feel good about what they're doing.

Physical anchors are used in combat: A touch on the shoulder while on patrol conveys much more than simple attention getting. Instantly, the warrior goes to full-alert status and is prepared for imminent action.

Verbal anchors can also be effective tools. One unsubtle verbal anchor is our national anthem, often used to motivate people by making them feel good, or as crowd control when fans get out of hand at ball games. Words such as *freeze* or *duck* transmit complete messages.

Parents often install verbal anchors in children, who know exactly what it means when a voice is raised or a certain tone employed. Verbal anchors can elicit both positive and negative states.

Installing verbal anchors is easy: Put the person in a receptive mood, then evoke the desired state. Next, use a specific word, phrase, or sound. If possible, repeat the process to strengthen the anchor. Later, you will be able to recreate that state by making the same sound again.

This technique is employed by hypnotists to implant a post-hypnotic suggestion that effortlessly reestablishes the hypnotic state. When we suggest the use of auditory or verbal anchors, we are *not* talking about inducing hypnotic states. Humans are in varying degrees of trance most of the time and are not aware of it. There is no pure trance state, as many commonly believe. Rather, there is a continuum of states of consciousness. During some of these, people are more amenable to influence from external sources. Anchors help evoke receptive states that enable you to influence others.

Have you ever bought a product from a glib salesperson and

later wondered why you bought it? Exceptional salespeople know many of these techniques. Some know how they influence others, but the majority have learned the process naturally, by trial and error. By studying and practicing the techniques discussed here, you can choose to influence others.

DIRECTION

People will tell you many useful things about themselves if you listen carefully. The direction of their motivation is one such thing. Direction indicates whether the person is motivated largely by positive or negative attractors. Knowing an individual's direction gives you an advantage when attempting to influence that person.

Some people work harder in pursuit of an attractive objective; others work harder to avoid an unattractive situation.

Advertising demonstrates how people can be negatively directed: If you don't use the right products, bad things will happen to you—your hair will fall out; your underwear will show; your teeth will rot; and you will smell bad, thus offending family and friends, who will be too embarrassed to tell you. If you don't buy the right insurance, and lots of it, you are willfully dooming your family in the event of your demise.

The advertising media have a clear understanding of strategy. By sowing the seeds of doubt, together with hard sell and the glitz of Madison Avenue, such marketing is uniquely successful.

There are several simple clues to the motivational direction of an individual: the person's occupation; goals; politics. Is he willing to take risks for his beliefs, or is he wedded to the status quo because it promises security? Even details such as the amount of traveling a person does may provide a clue to the degree of motivation. Remember that actions are a good barometer of the degree of commitment.

People motivated by positive attractors can be influenced by showing them a vision of what might be. They are not afraid to make mistakes or take calculated risks if the benefits are great enough. Such people will excel if presented with attainable yet challenging goals.

CHUNKING

When influencing people, it is useful to know how much detail a person needs or wants in order to process information. We refer to the processing of information in batches as chunking. A chunk consists of "any familiar unit, regardless of size, that can be recalled as an entity, given a single relevant cue."[15] The Preamble to the Constitution or Hamlet's "To be or not to be" soliloquy are "chunks" of information that people routinely commit to memory.

Some people require very complete details about a given situation, while others are comfortable with an overview. The former style connotes a micromanager; the latter, a laissez-faire individual.

Knowing how a person chunks information is important when you are presenting data. If you chunk too high (i.e., present an overview, assuming that the person will fill in the details), you risk seeming unprepared. On the other hand, including minute details deemed unnecessary may bore a bottom-line manager before you get to your desired outcome. The key here is pre-planning: Do your homework ahead of time, and *know your audience*.

A communication mismatch due to chunking differences marred meetings between former prime minister Begin of Israel and former president Ronald Reagan. As president, Reagan, who had a reputation for working in generalities, epitomized the laissez-faire manager: content to view the big picture, agree in principle, and let his staff fill in the details. Begin, on the other hand, wanted all the specifics on how agreements would be formulated and carried out. The two communicated very poorly.

Keep in mind that people file internal information differently. You may know some people who seem to remember names well and others who are better with dates or numbers. This is part of the functionality of chunking. There are five primary ways that people sort communication:

- people
- places
- activities
- information
- things

Try to determine what types of communication the person you wish to influence internalizes best. Again, active listening will provide you adequate clues. Does your target talk about people, places, things, or activities? What does he or she seem to remember well? Test your hypothesis in conversation by asking questions that require different sorts of responses.

When you need an answer or an approval from this individual, provide the data required for decision making in the way your target sorts it.

For example, if your target remembers people well, during a presentation, tell him or her about the people who are involved in the project. If the target remembers information, provide as much detail as the chunking level indicates he or she can absorb. The key is to communicate in the way the target prefers.

FRAMES OF REFERENCE
It is helpful, when applying the art of influence, to know whether the target uses an internal or external frame of reference.

Individuals with an external frame of reference worry about what others think. They are concerned about world opinion and how their actions will be viewed in a global context. They are likely to be self-protective, proponents of CYA—cover your ass. You may well find them avoidance-directed (i.e., motivated by negative attractors). On the positive side, externally motivated people care about the welfare of others and will take action to help, if it is socially acceptable.

Those with an internal frame of reference have a strong sense of right and wrong. They tend to moralize and are somewhat self-righteous. These people are primarily concerned with themselves and will manipulate interactions onto their own terms.

Another discriminator of value is the way a person deals with new data. People who have a low tolerance for ambiguity try to make sense out of new information by fitting it into their pre-existing model of reality. With such targets, try merging new data with similar, existing data, helping them see an existing pattern.

Other targets like to mismatch. People who use this method look for exceptions to the proposed rules. They take the rough edges and test them. They try to find out when the laws won't work. They ask questions that make you prove the viability of your proposal. A mismatcher will say, "Yes, but it won't work in case X." You must be prepared to explore those limits to such targets' satisfaction.

GROUP INFLUENCE

James G. Miller's living systems theory[16] explores the commonality of all living systems. He suggests that the acceptance of common values helps enhance group performance and reduce internal conflict.

These common values include: courage, candor, commitment, and competence. Commonly held values are not easily disrupted by external forces. They are even more deeply held than beliefs. The warrior trying to influence a group must be aware of the values and norms of the target group. If possible, the warrior should also help establish those values.

Secretary of the Army John Marsh declared 1987 the Year of Values. Throughout that year, common values were published and taught throughout the U.S. Army at all levels. This was an overt attempt to instill common values to all parts of the organization.

One military value is courage—courage under fire, in combat, and the courage to do what is believed to be right during peacetime. It has long been axiomatic that you don't leave your comrades—even if dead, and especially if wounded—when you are engaging the enemy. The knowledge that others will stay with you, even when faced with overwhelming odds, is what makes good fighting units great. Courage, like fear, is contagious, and allows individuals to do the impossible.

To influence an organization, you must understand its values. Sometimes they are openly stated; at other times they are less visible. Once the values have been determined, you should embrace them or at least appear to support them. Remember to keep your behavior flexible. Do periodic internal checks to maintain your own integrity. This is vital! Do not forget Polonius's admonition to the young Laertes: "This above all, to thine own self be true."

To determine the values of an organization, begin with its published literature. See what it is saying to the outside world. If you can access internal documents, compare them to external literature and check for consistency. Is what it says the same as what it does? Does it say the same things to the outside world as it says to its own people? The behavior of the organization tells you what its real values are.

Next, determine who holds power in the organization. Sometimes this is obvious by titles; sometimes it is not. Frequently, there is power behind the throne and you need to know where it lies.

When you are unsure of who is the real decision maker, there is a quick and easy way to find out. Once the group is assembled, ask a question such as, When should we have a break? or What does our timetable look like?

The person who answers, or whom the others look to, is the power broker. Watch to see whom he or she favors and how the others respond when questioned. The group dynamics will become readily apparent.

Once the group's power structure is clear, direct your attention to influencing the key member or members. The rest will usually fall into line very quickly.

Don't overlook what the military calls *horse-holders*. The term dates back to the days when senior officers had soldiers designated to hold their horses' bridles when they dismounted. While these people may be powerless on their own, they guard the gates to power and often can whisper in the "king's ear." They can get information to the seat of power or provide you with information. If slighted, they can be a major impediment to progress. Remember, eagles do not attack flies. Treat the palace guards with respect and they can be great allies.

Equally important to determining the power structure is knowing the golden rule: He who has the gold makes the rules. Frequently, much effort goes into attempting to influence a perceived power broker only to learn that he or she doesn't have access to the purse strings. Part of your initial assessment of the organization should include learning how funds are handled. This may vary greatly from organization to organization.

If the influence you wish to exert involves spending money, it is critical to understand the funding process. This can be very complex in large government organizations and confusing in smaller organizations. Be particularly sensitive to thresholds: dollar amounts that individuals are authorized to commit. Those figures will help you gauge the level of leadership you must influence to secure the desired funding level. That information may also guide you in putting together proposals to obtain funds. You may ask initially for an incremental amount to gain rapid approval and simultaneously plant a seed—the theory being, it's easier to get subsequent funding increases than to secure a large initial investment up front.

CLUES FROM THE ENVIRONMENT

The workplace often offers clues to an individual's value system. If possible, see the office of the person you wish to influence. If the target has no office, find an area that the target controls and evaluate the setting. What pictures are on the wall or desk? Are they job related, or of family and friends? Possibly they depict recreation or travel. These all reveal what is really important to that person. This examination helps provide an additional internal consistency check as to whether the individual and the organization hold the same values. Further, it assists you in determining how to approach that person with a proposal.

Examining an individual's work environment may tell you how that person processes information. Visually oriented people may have bright pictures. An auditorially dominant person may have sound equipment in the work space. A kinesthetic may have executive "toys" around. These clues can be tested along with your other observations.

When dealing with high-level executives, many more parameters come into play that must be evaluated. One of these is where the office is located. Corners are considered power spots. The relative power attached to an office is often directly proportional to its proximity to the penthouse suite. How big is the office? Size, when compared to other available offices, is often indicative of power. How many windows, if any, are there? How many phones are there? Who answers them? Do calls go through directly, even during meetings? If so, from whom? Who has the power to interrupt? Do husband, wife, or children get right through? Again, this is an indicator of values. How many secretaries are there? Do they interrupt? This is another indicator of the informal power structure. Where do you sit when meeting the executive? Does he come out from behind his desk or keep it between you? How big is the desk? What is it made of? What is the other furniture like? Are you sitting lower than the person you are meeting with? This is a subtle but oft-employed subliminal technique to establish the senior-subordinate relationship.

If you must wait to meet the executive, listening in the outer office can be informative. The waiting game itself can tell you much about how the executive views you and others. Power goes to the one who can keep the other waiting, and is sometimes employed as a test. Usually, you can discern between a genuine crisis causing a delay and pure impoliteness. What conversation goes on in the outer office? This can reveal as much about the organization's professionalism as it does about the respect the executive carries.

When meeting the executive, how is the introduction made? Are titles or first names used? Are you addressed by title or first name? If you have met previously, does the executive remember you? Does he know why you are there? If so, it tells you the visit is important enough that he was brought up to speed by the staff, or that the executive has an exceptional memory. Both are good signs.

Remembering the rule about flexible behavior, be prepared to accommodate the executive's expectations. Try to be what he or she desires you to be, in order to effectively achieve your purpose. However, don't violate your principles to do this. Preset limits on your behavior. Be willing to adjust, but only up to those limits. The bottom line in all influence interactions is integrity—for without it, you are lost.

4
THE JEDI PROJECT

In the late 1970s, a fictional class of warrior-monks captured the imagination of the world through the *Star Wars* films. The best of these Jedi were masters—individuals who, by rigorous training, had developed great physical and mental powers. Throughout the lore of history, such masters have epitomized the warrior's aspirations.

In 1983, the Jedi master provided an image and a name for the Jedi Project, a human-performance modeling experiment based on neuro-linguistic programming (NLP) skills. Sponsored by a U.S. government interagency task force, Jedi used advanced influence technologies to model excellence in human performance. The subjects involved in Jedi were willing to be influenced to acquire desirable skills.

The Jedi Project grew out of the New Patterns of Influence Program, developed during the early eighties to disseminate NLP skills throughout the U.S. Army, under the auspices of the U.S. Army Intelligence and Security Command and, until 1984, the Organizational Effectiveness School.

The number of human subjects involved in the Jedi Project was not statistically significant. The experiment was run as a proof-of-principle and, standing alone, the results are impressive.

Since insufficient funding existed to continue the experiment using a larger sample, we present these results to give you a look at the potential of these techniques, firm in our belief that this area demands additional research.

HISTORY

NLP itself was the first model for the Jedi Project.

NLP's creators, Richard Bandler and John Grinder, wanted to test their NLP theories by observing how behavior therapists function—why some therapists are very successful with patients making major behavioral transformations while others are not. Why do protégés of successful therapists employing the same procedures often fail to achieve comparable results?

Bandler and Grinder studied three "masters" in their respective fields: Fritz Perls, a renowned Gestalt therapist; Virginia Satir, a family therapist; and Erik Erikson, a master hypnotist. Bandler and Grinder observed the three in person and on videotape, then interviewed the therapists, closely questioning them on how they operated and what contributed to their success.

The resulting data, when analyzed, showed that certain techniques were independently employed by all three. These neurolinguistic-programming techniques became the foundation for the NLP program and later sparked the Jedi Project.

This research into modeling techniques determined the critical path for therapy. Critical-path method is an optimizing technique long employed in computer network analysis.[1]

The warrior defines critical path as the minimum number of steps required to accomplish a specific task. All tasks are accomplished in steps. Individuals may add extra steps, without realizing which steps are unnecessary, to achieve the desired result. The critical-path model catalogs all steps necessary to complete a specific task. Omitting even one of these steps prevents task accomplishment.

Although it is crucial not to omit steps, sometimes there may be reasons to add extra steps. You may not want to reveal the critical path, for reasons of mystique or covert purpose.

Beliefs may cause you to add steps. If observers believe that certain steps are critical, they may not accept your actions as complete if those steps are omitted. In shamanic healing, the shaman may give the patient a medicine that has curative powers or a placebo with no medicinal value. Either way, an elaborate healing ceremony accompanies the medicine. In some cultures, the ceremony itself is the curative agent and no drugs or placebos are used. These rituals elevate the patient's expectation. Without the expected rituals, the patient may not feel that he has received the full healing treatment.

In the Jivaro Indian culture of the Ecuadoran Andes, when a healing shaman cures a patient, he performs an all-night ritual in which he "sucks out" the essence causing the illness. This essence is represented to a patient by a magical dart that the shaman secretly puts in his mouth beforehand. The ritual climaxes when the shaman "vomits out the object and displays it to the patient. . . . To explain to the layman that he already had the objects in his mouth would serve no fruitful purpose and would prevent him from displaying such an object as proof that he had effected the cure."[2]

We shall see that belief still plays an active role in the modeling of skills.

MODELING CRITERIA
Under the auspices of Major General Stubblebine, a small interagency team (with the U.S. Army as the lead member) was formed to see if NLP modeling technology could be beneficially applied to real-world training problems. Since the U.S. military is the largest training institution in the world, much time and money could be saved by improving techniques for teaching common skills. This team was a part of a large-scale organizational look at training technologies.

As team members became familiar with NLP capabilities, they started wondering where its boundaries might be. They came to the conclusion that such boundaries existed only in the minds and belief systems of individuals. New and more complex skills will be required of our warriors in the future, and the project was an attempt to adapt training skills to meet these future needs.

The team's first task was to choose a skill that would be an acceptable test bed for the modeling technology. A broad range of skills was considered, based on the following criteria:

- Was the skill part of the standard Army training mission?
- Was the skill also employed by other organizations?
- Could the results be easily quantified?
- Could the results be reasonably extrapolated to other related skills?
- Was the skill normally taught in a short time (a few days)?
- Did the skill require both physical and mental components?
- Was the field already well researched?
- Were "masters" available to be modeled?
- Was the effort logistically supportable?

The team sought a skill that was important to all agencies involved, and one where quantified results would be easily accepted. The skill chosen to be modeled was .45 pistol shooting.

Marksmanship is important to military and law-enforcement agencies, and millions of dollars are spent annually on the training and maintenance of these skills. Anything that reduces training time or ammunition requirements, while maintaining or surpassing current training standards, is inarguably desirable. Marksmanship is also easily quantifiable—either you hit the target or you don't, and there is an established scoring system.

The team then did a comprehensive survey of the experts available to be modeled. All respondents, including police organizations and the National Rifle Association, agreed that the best source for experts was the Army Marksmanship Unit (AMU) at Fort Benning, Georgia. With the .45 pistol, these shooters were acclaimed as the best in the world.

The .45 pistol has been in the inventory since before the First World War. Although much is known about the characteristics of .45s, it is also known that there has been little improvement in its firing techniques in over fifty years. Granted, there have been mechanical advances, including tuning, better ammunition, and even laser and tritium sights, but the basics of firing a .45 remain the same.

In addition, the .45 has a well-established reputation for being hard to handle. Big men sometimes fear breaking a wrist or elbow from its legendary heavy recoil. Some shooters will tell you you're better off throwing a .45 at an assailant than firing it. Others swear by it and have no difficulty. Since the .45 met all the necessary criteria, marksmanship with this fabled weapon was selected as the first skill to be modeled.

THE "MASTERS"

The Army Marksmanship Unit agreed to provide its best shooters. The three selected masters included Master Sergeant Roger Willis, the national champion; Master Sergeant Max Barrington, the interservice champion; and their boss, Lieutenant Colonel Ralph Talbot, chief of the AMU pistol team and an expert in his own right.

On February 8, 1984, the shooters came to Arlington Hall Station, Virginia, home of INSCOM, where they were severely tested—both physically and mentally—for four days on the marksmanship range.

The three experts were questioned, separately and in detail, about their beliefs surrounding shooting. The modeling team soon learned that these experts had very positive views of shooting. They not only shot constantly at work, but they even shot recreationally on weekends. Shooting was their passion, not just their skill. They believed that shooting could save lives in combat, or during a robbery at home. They felt positively about their ability to save the lives of family or comrades.

Both master sergeants saw shooting as a way to make a good living. Each had spent many years on the AMU pistol team and only one year with regular troop units. Every day they went to the range and practiced shooting. This gave them great confidence in the capability of the .45 to hit the target consistently.

All three shooters grew up in times when defense of their country and military service were considered as virtues. The modeling team knew that those same sentiments might not be shared by new trainees.

As well as positive beliefs about shooting, each of the experts had great confidence in his own abilities. They knew they could shoot well, even when not in top form. They also knew from experience that if they got off balance, even by a little, muscle memory would act to correctly align their shot. They were so skilled that they trusted their bodies to do what they were trained to do: fire when they were on target, never throwing a round off target and losing all their points.

Each expert was asked to fire a number of rounds at a specific target. So that their eye movements could be safely observed, television cameras were placed in front of the shooters, slightly off center. The cameras were the safest and most practical way to collect data without being in front of the shooters.

After all the experts fired a number of rounds at their own pace, they were asked to vary their style by adjusting their physical stance. To determine the parameters of their physical capability, we asked them to shift their weight from right to left and front to rear; we changed their footing and asked them to fire while sighting with their weaker eye.

All shooters use a certain position, or stance. These experts used the classical "good form" stance long taught to marksmen. Altering that form confirmed that their belief in muscle memory was justified: They could extensively distort their normal physical firing position and still shoot accurately. Yet eventually these adjustments measurably affected their shooting.

The next step was to examine the experts' mental techniques. The expert shooters asked if drugs were to be used, because they had heard that the intelligence community employed drugs, and wanted no part of it. They were assured there would be no drugs of any kind.

Subsequent mental examination of the shooters made it apparent that each expert employed a very specific mental pattern. Each had received extensive training in internal visualization. Both of the sergeants went so far as to shoot the entire match in their heads the day prior to the match. This was not just a quick mental rehearsal of how to shoot a match. They fired *every shot* mentally, sometimes more than once.

These experts believed that shooting was 20 percent physical and 80 percent mental. They had specific, similar mental techniques that they employed while shooting. Each became one with the weapon. The gun was an extension of the shooter. *They let the bullet go down range—they didn't fire it.*

If this mental targeting was interrupted, their firing effectiveness was lost. Asked to perform a simple but mentally distracting task—such as humming "Mary Had a Little Lamb" while shooting—they immediately fell off target. This confirmed that mental targeting was the key to shooting accurately.

Although much of what the modeling team learned was predicted by theory, the expert shooters had a few surprises in store for us. The styles of the shooters varied considerably. One, when interrupted during his shooting cycle, would put the gun back in the case, take off his glasses, and start the entire cycle all over again—taking the gun from the case; loading it; putting on his glasses. This shooter had developed all match-related activities into an extensive ritual. The others could put the gun down, talk to you, pick up the gun, and begin again where they had left off, although one was quite casual about it, while the other was a bit more formal. There was a substantial variance in the amount of ritual behavior displayed by the three. These differences proved useful—remember, the modeling team was looking for the required critical path rather than embellishments a specific shooter might add for personal comfort.

The shooters found that they could not adequately describe how they learned to shoot or how each step in the shooting process was performed. As experts, they had chunked information into a reduced number of steps. The experts took many small pieces learned over a long period of time and condensed them into a single action or chunk: shooting. They successfully exported to unconscious memory all the supporting subcomponents of shooting necessary to achieve winning form.

Surprisingly, these experts do not need to hold their weapons perfectly still to shoot accurately. Under observation, the shooters displayed a great deal of arm movement as they were firing. They *mentally* controlled the trigger squeeze, and would not allow the bullet to "go down range" until their sights were on target. This mental control was an unconscious process that allowed trigger squeeze to occur only when the sights were aligned. The expert shooters call their technique "controlling the smallest arc of movement." They knew they would be moving and controlled the arc.

Attempting to make the shooters hold perfectly still proved counterproductive. They became tense, and the vibration in their arms increased to the point of uncontrollability.

THE MODEL

After two days of intensive work with the expert shooters, the task force took a day to synthesize the collected data. They then designed a universal shooting model that was transferable to other weapon systems.

The model involved elaboration of positive and negative beliefs about shooting; the analysis of physiological components involved in shooting; the design of a universally effective mental strategy for shooting.

This process revealed certain limiting beliefs about shooting that must be removed before they can be replaced with more appropriate ones:

· that firearms are "bad"
· that the .45 is an inaccurate and undesirable weapon
· that the .45 cannot be controlled because of its kick

- that one must hold the gun totally still to shoot bull's-eye
- that people cannot learn to shoot as an expert in two days

It was decided the beliefs of the experts should be installed in novice shooters. These included:

- It is good and natural to learn to shoot.
- Anyone willing to apply himself can become an expert, and that this can be accomplished quickly.
- Learning to shoot effectively may be an important tool for future survival.
- Shooting is a long-term and important job skill.
- Shooting may be for sport, for fun, and can carry prestige.
- Hitting the bull's-eye can be done naturally.
- The gun will fire without one's conscious effort when the sights are aligned.
- One becomes the weapon system—you and the weapon are one.
- Guns are safe but must be respected.
- Muscle memory may compensate for miscalculations.
- The shooter needs to be willing to try new approaches.
- Dry firing fifteen to twenty times before shooting will improve shooting scores.
- Shooting is mostly mental, "allowing" the biocomputer to do its thing.

Next, the important physiological components were outlined. These included:

- correct stance
- body posture
- muscle tone
- grip on the pistol
- arm position
- breathing
- sight alignment
- trigger pressure

The Jedi Project

The installation of mental strategies for successful pistol shooting includes mental rehearsal of all aspects of the shooting process and the physical rehearsal of the sequence followed by the expert shooters. The task force monitored the installation process to ensure that all trainees demonstrated, through repetition, the proper sequence of events to achieve success.

The critical piece in the installation process is the mental rehearsal of the sensory input, i.e., visual, auditory, and kinesthetic, in the proper sequence. Note that the trainees rehearsed all the mental aspects, not just visual ones.

Another key aspect to the mental process was to establish a success cycle. This meant that the first time the students fired, they were put into a situation that guaranteed success. For pistol shooting, this was accomplished by starting live fire at full-size targets at very close range—about ten feet. At that range, no one could miss and all experienced success from the start. This was a major departure from traditional training, where students begin at twenty-five meters and most of the early rounds miss the target. Nothing builds a better attitude as quickly as success.

Although success in hitting the target was the objective in this process, close-range shooting is not uncommon. Most police shootings take place at twenty feet or less, and most miss the intended target. The "pucker factor"—stress of combat so intense that your anus tightens—has something to do with this.

The critical path of the success cycle included reinforcing all mental aspects of shooting. The strategy for beginning shooters included:

- correct position and grip
- relaxation and taking a deep breath
- take up the slack (increase the tension) on the trigger
- visualization of perfect sight alignment
- concentration on the sight alignment
- application of steady trigger pressure and letting the gun go off
- recovery and preparation for the next shot
- internal auditory dialogue that supports the success sequence

The internal dialogue was modeled on what the experts said went on in their heads while they were shooting. All of the experts talked to themselves while firing. They repeated a mental chant: "breathe," "trigger slack" (or "get on the sights"), and "let the gun go off." Trigger slack is the distance the trigger can be pulled before it meets resistance. Once the trigger slack had been taken up, they switched between "sight alignment" and "let the gun go off," depending on their movement arc and the sight alignment.

To enhance shooting scores, the modelers made a few physical modifications. The front sights of the weapons were painted white to assist in directing the shooters' focus. This was done with the control group as well. They also placed a bright red dot in the targets' centers to help establish an aiming point.

A metronome was played throughout training to subconsciously install a sixty-beat-per-minute rhythm; this paid off when the trainees had to shoot a timed-fire course (five rounds within a prescribed period).

Once the task force determined the desired shooting model, they returned to the masters, describing the model and how they believed training should be conducted.

The response was immediate and enthusiastic. Participating AMU members felt this approach constituted a breakthrough in marksmanship training, possibly the first such breakthrough in a hundred years.

The Training Program

The next phase of the project was to translate the model into a training program that ordinary instructors could be taught to administer. A complicated training model that only NLP-trained experts could install would be useless to the average sergeant.

The task force was determined to teach the value of positive feedback. This would prove to be a challenge. Few combat-hardened NCOs go around spouting praise, no matter how good their men are. The NCO modus operandi of "kick ass and take names" is deeply ingrained as the official motivational philosophy.

To set a positive tone and demonstrate success, the AMU experts made a videotape. As you can see in the following excerpts from the script used by the Army trainer, the desired belief systems were embedded in a very positive way. The theme was: *This course is impossible to fail*.

"The pursuit of *excellence* in pistol shooting has been a life-long personal *commitment* of mine . . . a tradition as old and honorable as our Army itself. I am proud to be the man who welcomes and orients you to this expert training program, which will take you to total competency in pistol shooting in two days. This training is based on the actual performance of the finest pistol shooters in the USA. . . .

"During the next two days you will thoroughly learn their system and it will become your system for successful shooting. This training program is designed with the use of the most advanced technology available. This program has been consistently successful teaching people how to be successful in achieving their goals. It literally guarantees your success, regardless of your past beliefs. Within an hour, the army's two best pistol shooters improved their skills by applying this system, even though they've been shooting for more than twenty years. This is how powerful this training system is. Imagine what it can do for you. It is important that you allow yourself to learn. And you can and will learn. . . .

"Precision is also one of the themes of this training, both in the equipment, and in your ability to follow instructions. The .45 pistol is an accurate weapon, designed for personal defense. You will learn a step-by-step procedure which will enable you to deliver highly accurate fire on the target from a variety of positions. It is important that you pay attention and follow the instructions carefully. When you do this, success will be your reward."

Note the phrasing of the text. It is positively oriented, establishing a mental picture of success from the outset. This is very different from traditional training, stereotypically portrayed in films, where soldiers are browbeaten, told scatalogically how many will fail, and challenged not to be one of those failures.

Next, to test the new model of pistol shooting against the conventional system, we established two demographically balanced groups: a control group and a test group. All participants were young male and female service members. None was considered a pistol expert, though many had fired one in basic training or in civilian life. Weapons enthusiasts were screened out.

To ensure competent training for the control group, the AMU training unit, a team of expert shooters at Fort Meade, Maryland, was enlisted. The control group was trained on the Combat Pistol Qualification Course. The training period was four and a half days, and ended with the control group firing for the record.

The test group was trained over two days by two members of the original task force. Other members observed, but could not join the training process without upsetting the student-instructor ratio.

To minimize the Hawthorne effect (which states that any group singled out for special attention is likely to do better than a group doing the same task without special attention), both the control group and the test group believed that they were part of a demonstration singling them out as special. The control group was taught by the best available U.S. Army instructors. Therefore, the Hawthorne effect could reasonably be considered eliminated, since relative parity between the groups was established.

The test group watched the video, witnessed a demonstration, and then underwent a closed-eyes meditation during which the trainers installed positive beliefs about shooting. This closed-eyes process involved the use of the relaxation techniques discussed in Chapter 2, with music and a metronome in the background.

The soldiers were taught to visualize themselves as expert marksmen, using the visualization techniques you will learn in Chapter 7.

Following a safety briefing, weapons were issued to the test group. Physical contact between specific trainee and specific weapon was to be maintained throughout the training, to reinforce the concept of marksman and weapon as one complete system.

The control group took the traditional four-and-a-half-day course. In the traditional course, the introduction to weapons is slower. The shooter starts firing at a much greater range and invariably misses a large number of times. The students gradually learn to hit the target, but their first experience is usually failure, which must later be overcome.

The Results

The first firing for the test group was conducted the same afternoon, and most of the group qualified. An additional session was held the next morning, and by the end, all test-group participants had qualified in less than twelve hours of total training time.

The results of the training and firing for record are on the following page. Anecdotal test data worth noting included:

1) Two people from the test group qualified as expert after eight hours' training. Neither had ever qualified with a pistol previously. One was a female, the smallest and youngest member of that group. She reported that she had never fired a pistol before that day.

2) The test group allowed people to be released from training once they qualified on the second day. Experts were released at any stage.

There were several deficiencies the task force was aware of prior to and during the conduct of the demonstration. The test was designed as a feasibility study, to give a quick look at the techniques' potential. The parameters of this government project restricted the kind of money that was available: In order not to contravene the letter or the intent of restrictions imposed by Congress, research could not be conducted, but concepts for training could be tested.

Comparison of the Control and Test Groups

	Control Group (1)	Test Group (2)	Ratio of Test / Control Group
Length of training	3½ days (27 hours)	1½ days (12 hours)	0.44
% of personnel qualified	8/11 73%	12/12 100%	1.37
Points per person	292.7	295.9	1.01
Hits per person	35.6	36.3	1.02
% of experts	10%	25%	2.50
Average rounds per person to qualify	375	176	0.47

Demographic Comparison

	Control		Test	
	Range	Average	Range	Average
Age	20–34	23.8	19–37	23.16
Grade	E2–E6	E4.08	E1–E6	E4.1
GT Score	92–143	113.8	69–139	105.75
	Attend	Qualify	Attend	Qualify
Male/Female	9/2	7/1	11/1	11/1

The number of participants was very low; therefore the sample size was not statistically significant. It was always maintained that a follow-up study employing thousands would be required to validate the study.

Two different firing ranges were used. This was not the design of the study but occurred when the range scheduled for both groups to fire on failed to operate adequately. Considering temperature, lighting, and other climatic factors, it was not considered to be a fatal flaw.

No baseline measurement was taken. This was a conscious decision prior to the demonstration. It was felt that firing a baseline round would severely impact the attempt to create a situation where the student never experienced failure. This was compensated by establishing a matched-pair sampling technique.

The control group did not fire for record prior to its final day. The choice was made to test against the published, existing, system as opposed to any modification.

Despite potential criticism, the pistol-shooting portion of the Jedi Project was a success. The intent of this preliminary study was to determine whether this NLP modeling technique warranted further study. It demonstrated that in a short period of time, experts could be modeled and a training program developed to enhance the skills of trainees, using techniques that could potentially save scarce training resources, ammunition, and time.

ADVANCED MODELING TECHNIQUES

The biggest success of the Jedi Project was the development of a universal modeling process applicable to most skills. Those principles can be used to achieve success in the area of your choice.

Once you have chosen your skill and your master(s), you will employ the following process:

1. Elicit the beliefs of the expert.
2. Model the pertinent physiology.
3. Determine the limits of physiology.
4. Model the mental strategy.
5. Form a tentative generalization regarding the beliefs, physiology, and mental strategy of the experts.
6. Mold someone (possibly yourself) to fit the model.
7. Review, test, and refine the training model.
8. Implement refinements and install the final model.

The most important component of modeling is your ability to observe. The vast majority of people rely on gross generalities and casual observation to learn what is going on around them. They see only what they want, expect—or fear—to see.

When modeling, you must be open to new possibilities if you are to be successful. *Assume* that the expert has something to teach you and that you know nothing of how he or she achieves results. Watch and listen carefully.

Watch a child modeling an adult. Have you ever noticed a father and son walking together? See how similar their walks really are. Children learn by closely watching everything adults or older children do, then modeling the observed behaviors.

Since the key to modeling is observation, your ability to make quality observations of the master you wish to model is vital. Remember to constantly cross-check your observations with the other available data.

Beliefs and Values

It is important that you understand the beliefs motivating the master or expert you have chosen to model. You can elicit beliefs in several different ways.

The simplest approach is to come right out and ask the individual questions about the beliefs and attitudes toward the skill to be modeled. If possible, make contact with more than one expert, and compare their responses.

In modeling, we say that behavior is believable. In other words, watch what people do; what they say is less reliable. Watch for internal consistency between what experts do and what they say they do. Cross-check by asking the same question differently. Is the response the same, or at least internally consistent?

If so, you probably have a good reading of that expert's beliefs. If not, keep probing until you have what you need.

If direct access to your chosen expert(s) is unavailable, there may be other sources of information at your disposal. Obtain copies of any books and articles written by the expert. Try to determine if the material was written personally or if a staff or ghost writer was employed. In either case, the expert was in control of the finished product; it is his public persona. Therefore, he endorses that view of himself.

Find out why the material was written, if you can. Knowing the target or the intended audience can be key to understanding the material's relevance to your model.

Finally, if the expert is newsworthy, there may be additional material on film or video. This is particularly handy when it comes to modeling the physical aspects of the skill involved.

You may be in a position to make your own videos of the expert, either overtly or covertly (although we recommend you use the latter only as a last resort and within the bounds of law, reason, and privacy). The availability of this type of asset should be a serious consideration when choosing the experts to be modeled.

Physiology

The physiological parameters of the skill you choose to model can vary tremendously. High physical skills would include most sports. An example of high mental skills would be to model the analytic processes of top scientists or engineers.

Once you have determined which skill you want to model and the level of effort you wish to commit to the project, consider the attributes of the experts to be modeled as well as your own. If you are forty years old and weigh 160 pounds, you might think twice about modeling a linebacker from the New York Jets—unless of course you happen to play in an over-the-hill league somewhere.

If you are working closely with the experts, have them show you how they hold and move their bodies. If given the opportunity for this kind of close relationship, ask them to change their normal patterns. As they do this, test the limits of their capability by having them gradually change their position while they practice the skill you want. Determine the points at which the experts start to seriously degrade their skills due to these deviations. Where is the expert's center of gravity? What happens if that is moved? Watch the entire body. Where is the head placed and how is it carried? What are the positions of the hands and feet? When do they shift? What happens if another grip or position is used?

Watch closely when the experts are performing. Do they really do what they told you to do? When do things go wrong? Under what conditions? What were the differences between the times when the skill went perfectly and the times it slipped even a small amount?

You are looking for the difference that makes a difference: what separates the experts from the good performers. A way to determine physiological differences is to take both video and still photography of the experts performing their skill. Now, obtain photos of good or average participants performing the same skill. Compare the two.

In addition to how experts perform their respective skills, also examine how they train. This may provide insights into the basic skills needed to maintain and support expert performance, as well as a model training program.

Another point of inquiry is what the entry-level skills and capabilities of the experts were. This is important if you are in a position to hire or train others to do specific tasks. Determine what particular entrance skills are required, or at least establish a pattern that will help you hold down a washout rate, since training dollars are an expensive investment for any organization.

Mental Strategy

The mental strategy an expert employs with any skill, no matter how simple, is a key factor in the modeling process. Humans are creatures of habit, and they create patterns even though they may not recognize them. Experts are no different. In fact, they may be even more driven by patterns. They have learned what works for them and have been rewarded for that skill. While they may make minor modifications on rare occasions, generally they will stick to proven patterns of success.

In the .45 pistol shooting, certain mental characteristics were common to all the experts modeled. In addition, when their train of thought was broken, their shooting quickly degraded. The ability to concentrate on the task is common to most of the skills modeled so far. The trick is to find the key elements of the mental strategy employed.

With direct access, you can ask the experts what they are

thinking about when they are performing each element of the skill. Record what they tell you they think about *prior to performance*. Then have the experts go through the skill and again state their thoughts *during* each stage of the action. Compare what they told you in both sessions. If you have several experts, capture all their expressions. Remember, you are looking for the critical path, not the most complete set of thoughts.

An additional skill you can practice while extracting the mental strategy again comes from influence technology. Observe the experts' eye-movement patterns and implement them during this phase. With some practice, you will be able to quickly calibrate the experts' eye patterns. You then want to check what is being said versus the eye movements for consistency. If they talk about what they are hearing but seem to be accessing pictures in their heads, just note it. Then ask questions about what they *see*.

Do not challenge the experts. If you do so, they are likely to cut you off from the data you need. Just note any inconsistencies, catalog them for later analysis, and be sure to observe other experts closely at the same stage of the strategy elicitation. Remember, you are looking for the critical path, i.e., what works for all the experts.

When working with the experts, you may be able to test the limits of their mental strategy. Try interrupting them and observing how they respond. Do they simply stop and then proceed, or do they recycle back into an earlier part of the program? If they recycle, how far back do they go? Is it as far as the pistol shooter who put his weapon back in the case, or merely a couple of subelements in the process?

How the experts respond to interruption is also important. Do they respond civilly, or does the interruption elicit an emotional outburst? This sometimes occurs when experts are deep in concentration and have blocked out the external world. Try to determine the level of attention modelers must factor in when designing training programs.

An example of a successful elicitation of an internal mental strategy comes from a study of Stinger missile shooters. The Stinger is a ground-to-air shoulder-fired missile designed to protect front-line troops in combat. It is quite costly to build, and gained a lot of credibility when it was introduced into Afghanistan, where it changed the balance of power by seriously degrading Soviet air superiority. A study was conducted by Bob Klaus and Wyatt Woodsmall, both of whom were important members of the Jedi Project. They observed both training and live firing and interviewed the top shooters. The strategy they elicited was as follows:

- Review the firing sequence.
- Perform tasks for readiness to fire.
- Acquire the target (gunner sees target).
- Listen for tone acquisition (which tells the gunner the target is in range and locked on).
- Determine target (identify friendly or unfriendly).
- Feels right? (a kinesthetic check).
- Fire.

While this sequence is specific to the Stinger, it does bring up a step that appears in several models requiring action. This is the "feels right," or kinesthetic, internal check. Other shooting skills, and sports such as basketball and baseball, have this "K" check. When things go well, players talk of being "on" and knowing that their actions feel right. When they talk of being "off," they realize it was some internal kinesthetic problem.

If the skill to be modeled is in the cognitive domain, the mental strategy may be less observable. Still, it is there and obtainable.

What successful salespeople have is the ability to close the sale. Their strategy is to achieve rapport with their clients, gain their confidence, and then close the sale. The internal mental strategy of the successful salesperson may be to rehearse the entire sequence before meeting with the client; closely observe the client during the contact; adjust his or her style to coincide with the client's preferred interaction style; enter the client's comfort zone; elicit the client's decision-making strategy, and then move on to closing the sale. Often, they use the internal K check. If the K check is negative, the super-salesperson knows that continuing to introduce new points or trying to build more rapport, sometimes known as bullshitting, may lose the sale.

Modelers have noted there is a strong connection between physiology and internal kinesthetics. This should be remembered when attempting to model any skill. There really is a posture of excellence.

In advanced NLP training, the linkage between physiology and internal kinesthetics became clear. Under certain conditions, one could establish an exact physical configuration and use it to elicit emotional response in others. The process could even be used to change an individual's personal history and make him and others believe the new history.

Forming Generalizations

It is time to start to build your model. Take the data you have collected and search for underlying patterns. The critical path will gradually emerge.

Ask yourself a series of questions. What are these experts saying and doing in common? What are their belief systems? What do those belief systems have in common that support their ability to accomplish extraordinary things? What is the difference that makes a difference?

Once you have answered these questions, make a list. Subdivide the categories of data into beliefs, physical and mental. Arrange the data so that you can view all of it at once. Use butcher paper, large chalkboards, or perhaps a computer with a spreadsheet program such as Lotus 1–2–3.

The simplest technique is to use butcher paper. You will need space to hang the paper so you can see all the data at one time. Then any patterns will stand out plainly. Use large felt-tipped pens, and write down everything said about beliefs and values. Quote the experts, don't rephrase into your words. This may be important in detecting unconscious beliefs. It will also serve to keep out your own biases as much as humanly possible. Write the statements using short phrases. This should not look like an essay but a series of bullets or one-liners.

Next, step back and look at what you have written. Specifically, look for common words and themes various experts have used. Work to both include and exclude statements. If you find a single statement from an expert that is contradicted or neglected by other experts, it is probably not an important supporting belief. Whenever you see the same words being used over and over by more than one expert, take note. Use colors to circle or underline the common ideas. Draw lines connecting the statements.

An example of a belief that supported a skill, but was not intuitively obvious, came from the Stinger firing. Because it was a high-priced weapon, very few gunners ever got the opportunity to fire a live round. For expert gunners, the supporting belief was that it was an honor to be assigned as a Stinger gunner. This was elicited from interviews with several expert gunners. The belief that selection as a Stinger gunner was an honor conferred a sense of responsibility and an expectation of success. It worked.

Once you have determined your best estimate of the supporting beliefs, attempt to list them in their respective priority: which of the beliefs and values observed are of high importance; which are of relatively low importance.

After completing your analysis of the belief-and-value-system data, repeat the process using the information collected on the physiology supporting successful skill accomplishment by listing your observations and evaluations. Note the commonalities of the physiology as well as the differences. How far can the experts distort their position before significantly degrading performance? What are the common factors all agree on as being important? With pistol shooting, all agreed the grip and trigger squeeze were most important. The experts could be off balance and still compensate, but they couldn't have a loose grip and shoot well. List the key physiological factors.

Finally, using the elicited mental strategies of the experts, form a hypothesis about what is going on inside their heads as they are performing their skill.

Once you have developed a test of generalizations about how the experts successfully accomplish their tasks, if possible, ask the expert's opinion of your hypothesis. Be ready to alter your hypotheses on a proposed change if the majority of the experts concur. You are looking for the best model, not defending your idea of the way you think things should be done.

Last but not least, do a reality check. Before accepting or rejecting changes from the experts, determine if the proposed changes make sense. Early modeling efforts indicated the experts often don't fully or consciously know *how* they do so well. If proposed changes are radical, you may want to test two versions and determine "what works."

Testing the Model

Now that you have formed your generalizations about how the experts accomplish their task, it is time to test these generalizations. You need to find someone who is willing to try out your proposals. You may be the best person to do this. You know better than anyone else what was really formed in your mind. By doing it yourself, you minimize the risk of errors in translating the model into reality. However, you may get caught up in the modeling effort and miss some points about why an aspect of the model worked or didn't work.

Group efforts work best. Have the test candidate mold himself or herself to the model you have derived from your generalizations. Start by reviewing the beliefs and values supportive to the accomplishment of the skill involved. Next, duplicate the physical aspects and teach the candidate the internal mental strategy elicited.

The tester must set aside any preconceptions in conflict with the hypothesized set. Be willing to explore and see "what works." Allow the tester to determine whether or not the new set of beliefs and values is more supportive than the old set.

In modeling, you must be flexible if you want to influence others. If you could do the task as well as the experts, you probably would not be going through the modeling process. You are looking for the difference that makes a difference. This means you must be willing to entertain flexibility of mind and body.

To test the physical characteristics of the experts, it is best to have at least two people involved. One will act as the model and the other a critical observer. Both should be familiar with the model you are testing, and should have observed the experts performing their skill. The tester should then replicate the act or actions of the experts by following the hypothesized model as closely as possible.

It is the task of the observer(s) to evaluate the testers' performance and to assist in corrections as necessary. These corrections may be either to the testers' actions or to the model. At this point, you want to make only minor modifications to the model. If you find the hypothesized model does not work, you will need to reevaluate your observations or perhaps your generalizations. Testing the model should make it clear where you have strayed.

Once you are able to emulate the experts' physiology, it is time to install the internal mental strategy. Memorize the mental strategy. Know implicitly when to employ each phase of it. Go over the strategy several times verbally. Have the observers review your rehearsal for correctness. Repetition is critical if the strategy is to be internalized, sublimated, and automatic.

Have the mental strategy written in large letters on butcher paper and hung within view. This will provide the tester confidence, knowing it is there for reference if necessary.

Once all aspects of the model have been put together—i.e., beliefs, physiology, and mental strategy—the model has become testable.

The bottom line is whether or not the tester is able to accomplish the skill and how well. If the tester is attempting a skill previously performed, you have a baseline from which to measure. Did the performance increase? If so, how much? Can the model be improved? What aspects of the model are most helpful? Which, if any aspects, detract? How closely did the tester emulate the experts?

Prior to conducting your test, you should establish the criteria for success and how it will be measured. This definition will prevent observers from detracting from your results. If your program is being done for others to evaluate, be sure you come to agreement on the definition of success and measurement techniques *prior* to conducting the test. Even if you are just doing the modeling to improve your own skill in a particular area, you should establish preset goals and guidelines.

If the model improves skill performance, keep it. If modifications need to be made, adjust accordingly and retest. Stay with what works.

Designing Training

You are now at the point where you have a successful model of the skill you have chosen. If this is a personal skill you wish to improve, practice. Practice refines skills.

If you wish to transfer the modeled skill to others, you must standardize the teaching process. In the pistol-shooting example, it was important for the model to be teachable to an average noncommissioned officer, the real trainers of the Army. The requirement was for a program, transferable to NCOs, that could efficiently teach new soldiers to shoot more effectively.

This requirement limited the modeling. The skills had to be relatively simple to transfer. The model could not require extensive training in NLP. If the proposed model required extensive retraining of the NCO instructors, the result would have amounted to exchanging one training problem for another. Therefore, a program was designed that required very little new training for the NCOs. The mission was to reduce training time overall.

To develop any new training program, you first need to know the current method of instruction, the current trainers, and the level of investment in the existing training program.

Avoid turf battles as much as possible. Outside consultants seem to threaten the well-being of established groups. Current instructors often feel that, because they have been at the task a long time, they know the best way to get the job done.

You must be willing to enter this training environment and make the results so attractive to the instructors that they become enthusiastic about the new approach. This can be accomplished by making it "their program."

Otherwise, coming into an organization as the experts from out of town, you may well be seen as opponents to be defeated. Establish a plan to overcome local resistance and gain acceptance and assistance as quickly as possible.

Implementing the following principles during program development will minimize difficulties:

- Know the instructor's beliefs and values.
- Know the current training program.
- Make your program as compatible with the experts' as possible.
- Demonstrate results.
- Show how your program was derived.
- Minimize the amount of new skills the instructors must learn.
- Get instructors to accept your logic.
- K.I.S.S.—keep it short and simple.

Make the new training program attractive to the instructors by showing them how the experts benefitted from your modeling.

In pistol shooting, the experts were undisputed champions. To assist in training both instructors and students, a training video was made. It gave the experts the opportunity to say, in their own words, "This process works." If you have the open endorsement of one or more expert, this establishes your credibility.

Once you have established credibility and demonstrated a

better way to perform a skill, the instructors may be ready to listen. If so, allow them to participate in developing the training program.

In developing the program, keep in mind the chunking rule: People can remember seven, plus or minus two, chunks of information at any given time. If you are establishing lists of subtasks to be performed, keep them down to seven elements.

If you find too many subelements to be performed, you have two options available. First, you can combine subelements into a single, larger grouping. The experts may have already done this for you. Frequently, they think of a complex task as a single element. If feasible, use their chunks. Second, break the training into subcomponents. This will afford you the opportunity to teach each of the identified elements at any given time. Once the subcomponents have been mastered, assemble them into a comprehensive program that results in performance of the total skill.

One key element in all workable training programs is the success cycle. In pistol shooting, this was accomplished by shooting the targets at very close range. From the very beginning, the student was able to hit the target and experience success. In conventional training programs, emphasis is on "difficult," and the students believe it.

To build in the critical path of your success cycle, start the student on a task, any task, at which he or she cannot fail. Then build on that task to the more complex skills. The presupposition is that everyone succeeds at this course. Start at reduced ranges, slower speeds—whatever applies to the skill you wish to teach.

In addition to the success cycle, see to it that every participant is rewarded. Build a reward system into the training. It may be praise from the instructor, applause from classmates, or more formal recognition such as trophies, badges, or certificates.

While using the reward system, have your instructors constantly think and act in a positive fashion. This is no small task. Many individuals have grown up in environments of negative reinforcement, programmed by segments of society to look at things negatively.

This negatively-based thinking process comes from hierarchical traditions established in our society. We always strive to be "better than." There are two ways to become better than. One is to be positive and achieve the best we can. The other is to demote someone else and make him or her "less than," thereby establishing our relative position above the person. Unfortunately, it is easier to tear down than it is to build, and we too frequently rely on the negative approach to position establishment. This entire frame of thinking is deleterious to the concept of promoting excellence.

Certainly, within the military, the senior-subordinate relationship has been portrayed in the extreme. We have all seen the motion-picture drill instructor telling the bungling recruit he is a lower life form and doesn't deserve to exist in the same service. This demeaning attitude still prevails in many sectors and is very hard to displace. In fairness to the services, they have been trying for a long time to reverse this trend, although the tradition does not die easily.

The beauty of the success-cycle approach is that it offers a critical path on which all can succeed. There are an abundance of good things and they are available to all, not just a few. All success-oriented training programs should provide for the ability of every participant to succeed. Even those who are not as successful in attaining the skills sought may be redirected in a positive way. They are not failures; they are people whose talents lie in another area.

Refining the Training Model
Once you have trained your cadre of instructors, conduct a training session. This will be another check of the training program, as well as verification that you have successfully transferred the desired teaching skills to those instructors.

You have predefined measures of success. Check the results of training against the prior results. Is there a quantifiable difference? In what area? To what is the change attributed?

Based on your evaluation of these and similar methodological questions specific to your skill, further refine your training program and the techniques employed by your instructors. Gather data from students about the training process. What was helpful? What impeded learning? Did the instructors deliver the training as designed or revert to old techniques?

Implement and Install the Model

Once you have been through a few training cycles, you will have a good sense of your model's effectiveness. When you are getting consistently good results, it is time to release the model into the normal training system and search out a new area in which to excel.

Modeling can be a powerful tool that allows us to focus on excellence. Modeling based on expert performance can enhance the acquisition of complex skills.

For the average trainee, modeling provides a path to excellence. Modeling can increase performance in most skills: in cooking, typing, the driving of cars or motorcycles, sailing, hunting, and team sports, as well as stock brokerage, creative arts, component design, and martial arts.

In lieu of a personal mentor, in our modern world—where apprenticeships are nearly unknown in the traditional sense—modeling allows any motivated individual to access and transfer the skills of those most gifted individuals in a chosen field wherever those experts reside.

For an individual, a business, or a government organization, modeling is the true path to excellence. For exceptional students, it provides the chance to become the pathfinders of tomorrow.

5

CHARTING COURSES: REALITY MAPPING

One of the most successful recruiting campaigns ever launched by the U.S. military establishment used the now-familiar theme "Be all that you can be." This theme implicitly promises that through your military experience, you can realize your full potential.

Reality mapping allows individuals, organizations, and nations to use belief systems to chart a path through the universe. A reality map is a set of conceptual boundaries that determine the limits of expectation, what is—and is not—possible in a particular belief system.

For years, the Western nations were perceived by nondemocratic nations as "capitalist warmongers," and the socialist nations were viewed by the West as "communist hegemonists." Each thought the other was trying to swallow the globe entirely, and the cold war was the result. On the reality map of Western nations, half the world was lost. On the reality map of the socialist republics, a great and threatening enemy loomed.

The reality map of the two superpowers, although in no way physical, determined behaviors and spent lives for metaphors in decades of war.

REALITY MAPS SHAPE THE WORLD

Around 1300 B.C., a Hittite king used his reality map and the excuse of a timely eclipse to declare a politically meddlesome queen guilty of witchcraft and have her executed, in accordance with the belief system of his people.

Homeric Greeks never sailed out of sight of land in their long ships; they hugged the coast, because their reality maps told them that any seagoing ship would be lost and their belief systems peopled the sea with deadly sirens, monsters, and gods.

In the time of Alexander the Great, when his archrival, the Persian king Darius, wanted to cross a river with his army, the entire army stopped while the king threw hot manacles into the river and disciplined it according to the reality map of the day. If the river gods were not beaten and shamed into submission, said the belief system of the Persian army, any attempted crossing would end in disaster.

For centuries, European sailors navigated by reality maps that unequivocally stated that the world was flat; if you sailed too far, their belief systems said, you'd fall off.

Columbus's reality map told him he'd found India when he landed in the New World; his accomplishment changed belief systems all over the globe.

When America began developing the atomic bomb, a group of concerned scientists presented well-researched papers saying that the first atomic detonation would set the earth's atmosphere on fire; their reality map was proved wrong at Trinity Site.

The wrong reality map can kill you, because your reality map sets your expectations. The right reality map can free you, vindicate you, or make you a hero. For individuals, nations, and cultures, all empowered by belief systems, reality maps are often the place where history is made and fates decided.

Changes in national reality maps rock the world when they occur. Gorbachev's *perestroika* is one example.

Janet Morris offers another: In the early 1980s, General Danny Graham was advocating a reality map of mutually assured survival through space-based defense, then called the

High Frontier. As the concept developed, its name was changed to ballistic missile defense.

Morris was asked by Dr. J. E. Pournelle, of the Citizen's Advisory Committee on Space, to prepare one of a group of papers destined for Judge William Clark, then Ronald Reagan's national security adviser, analyzing the impact ballistic missile defense (BMD) might have on America's future.

Her paper was entitled "Ballistic Missile Defense: Will BMD Make Nuclear Weapons Obsolete?" In it, she projected an American reality map including BMD that would bring the Soviets back to the bargaining table, stress them economically, cause interim problems with our NATO allies and perhaps even some short-term escalation in the arms race, but in the end be beneficial to all. Whether the start-up hardware worked or not, Morris suggested, was unimportant. By changing the strategic expectations of the superpowers from mutually assured destruction to mutually assured survival, we might change a worldwide belief system fixated in horror on the specter of nuclear war.

Reagan's subsequent "Star Wars" speech officially christened BMD as the strategic defense initiative (SDI) and ignited international controversy.

Aside from doubts as to whether Reagan's reality map could be made practical with functioning defensive systems, many scientists Morris knew expressed serious moral reservations about working on such projects. Some found it difficult to decide whether SDI fit their belief systems, asking both Can it be done? and Should it be done?

Today, strategic-defense hardware is still in design and test phases. But the reality map has already changed many belief systems, in and out of government. Some in the intelligence and defense communities credit the strategic defense initiative with catalyzing *perestroika* and stabilizing, if not decelerating the nuclear and conventional arms races.

The power of this new reality map, which includes the possibility of a future free of nuclear nightmares, is unequivocal. Like the changing realities of international politics themselves, it is accepted more or less fully at different levels of understanding, according to the belief systems of individuals. But the reality map has changed, and the world will never be quite the same.

THE INDIVIDUAL REALITY MAP

Your collection of values—those things and qualities you have chosen to label good and worth emulating—have helped you organize a belief system that filters data from the outside world. This belief system defines good and bad, moral and immoral, for you. The scope of your belief system can never exceed that of your reality map, because possibilities that do not exist on your reality map are unbelievable and therefore out of reach. For instance, if you can never imagine yourself earning more than thirty thousand dollars a year, it is likely you never will.

The reality map of a nation defines its character and charts its destiny. Your reality map comprises the boundary conditions of your personal universe. It defines for you what is possible and impossible. It is the reference system you use to determine whether a phenomenon is real or unreal—or whether an event is an act of God, a trick of fate, or a simple coincidence.

Science teaches us to be clinical and objective, to deny noncausal phenomena. But if your belief system includes faith and your reality map includes a higher, ordering force, then you may find power available to you that is denied to others.

THE WARRIOR'S REALITY MAP

The warrior has a stringently crystallized reality map, for the warrior *must* believe in some higher truth. There are no atheists in foxholes.

The modern soldier relies on established tactics and firm beliefs when confronted with a life-threatening situation: He does what he has been trained to do.

When training fails and reason is insufficient to save the day, the warrior reaches deep within, where his fundamental vision of self, God, or the universe provides the winning edge. But those beliefs must already be there. Combat is no place to be making major adjustments to your belief system. In a critical situation, where even the slightest hesitation may prove fatal, the warrior counts on his readiness to improvise, survive, and win.

The warrior shapes his own destiny. He defines the limits of his own possibilities. He creates his own luck.

MAKING YOUR REALITY MAP WORK FOR YOU:
POINT MAPPING

It is time to see what expanding your reality map might do for you.

On a blank sheet of paper draw a point, or locus. This will represent your current position in reality—a point of departure.

All about you is empty space, the uncharted potential that contains everything you desire.

Draw a second point. Let this point represent a specific goal, achievement, or destination. Take care how far you place it from the first point; the farther away, the longer it will take to get there.

Since all great journeys begin with a single step, make an interim dot, nearer your current position, and call it step one of the journey you intend.

Now you have established a scale of distance you must cover—or effort you must expend—to reach your destination.

Knowing your direction, the distance to your final destination, and the length of a single step, draw incremental dots representing necessary steps along the route you intend to take. Now label each dot with the interim goal it represents.

If you doubt that you are planning a *real* trip, consider what has been going on in your mind thus far: Anyone—almost anyone—can draw dots on paper. Only a mind intent on accomplishing a desired objective can create a detailed itinerary representing a course of action leading to a desired result.

At the mind's subjective dimension you already know *who*'s going where and even *how far* you are from your goal. Your imagination has filled in all the blanks. It always will if you let it.

Now, envision the terrain underlying the points you have drawn. Perhaps there is a yawning chasm between two of your steps, or a desert to cross, an ocean, glacier, volcanic spill, or hostile horde. Or perhaps your journey offers distractions, beautiful vistas, hidden treasure, infatuations. Obstacles come in all flavors. Make a logistical analysis of the operation you are planning, including worst-case scenarios.

The invisible factor on the map is time . . . no respecter of dreams. All operational goals are time dependent. Ally yourself to action; resist inertia. If you want to get where you're going, stack the odds; leave early. The axiom is: Perfect preparation prevents poor performance.

Now, return to dot number one—you.

Mapping your reality is a surefire technique for getting yourself off the conceptual dime. Get going, keep going, and let your desire and imagination fill in the blanks.

There's a dot out there with your name on it.

To prove it, we're going to teach you to find out all you need to know about what you want and what you'll do to get it.

SYNCHRONICITY

Synchronicity is a term coined by the eminent psychologist Dr. Carl Gustav Jung to describe separate and apparently unconnected events possessing a hidden connectedness.

Jung described this acausal connecting principle as a "psychically conditioned relativity of space and time."[1] A synchronistic event may be as simple as a meaningful coincidence—if that coincidence is well beyond the bounds of probability.

Long before Jung, brilliant minds wrestled with the implications of synchronicity. In ancient Greece the Presocratic philosopher Heraclitus of Ephesus was widely quoted—by Plutarch, Hippolytus, and others—as having said, "An unapparent connection is stronger than an apparent." Wisdom, Heraclitus believed, was to "know the thought by which all things are steered through all things."

Jung's synchronistic events display a "falling together in time, a kind of simultaneity." "[. . .] a coincidence in time of two or more causally unrelated events which have the same or similar meaning. . . ."[2]

The warrior who is sensitive to synchronicity can generate luck. A synchronistic event is noncausal, coincidental, and recognizably good or bad in human terms—either lucky or unlucky: the "simultaneous occurrence of a certain psychic state with one or more external events which appear as meaningful parallels to the momentary subjective state. . . ."[3]

Acausal synchronistic phenomena include:

1. a psychic state in the observer that corresponds to a simultaneous external event with no causal connection between the two;

2. a psychic state that corresponds to an external event occurring at a distance from the observer and only verifiable after the fact;

3. a psychic state coincidental to a corresponding future event only verifiable at a later date.

To harness synchronicity, the warrior must become a focus of coincidence. Simple coincidence may be chance. Multiple coincidences linked by correspondence and interconnectedness are called luck—unless one is consciously trying to generate such coincidences. A researcher generating such coincidences in a laboratory under controlled conditions is doing research on the quantum mechanics of consciousness and the effect of mind on probability.

The individual who applies the same techniques to life is using the warrior's edge to make synchronicity an ally. We're making those techniques available to you. The warrior manipulates coincidence to create luck. As any warrior knows, it doesn't matter how good you are if you aren't lucky.

THE TARGETING LIST

In early 1989, Janet Morris phoned John Alexander, saying, "John, I need a little logistical help . . ." and trailed off, uncertain of her reception.

Alexander immediately asked, "What's the target?"

One of the most powerful tools in the warrior's arsenal is the targeting list. All three of us have been using this technique for years. In the military, as in business, versions of the targeting list pop up as agendas, operational scenarios, and strategic and tactical planning memoranda. In personal life, the targeting list is just as important.

On a sheet of paper, make a list of what you wish to accomplish in life, in order of importance, with item number one being the most important entry. The list may be as long or as short as you wish and as detailed.

Make some items on the list time specific by saying, By such and such a date, I will have accomplished such and such goal.

Show your list to no one. Memorize it. Read or recite it upon awakening, before bedtime, and any other time it occurs to you to do so.

When you are reciting your list, if you realize that some entries are not in the correct order of importance, rewrite the list and rememorize it. Whenever a goal on your list is achieved, reconstruct the entire list with as much care and thought as you took the first time you wrote it.

Don't be afraid to put on your list extremely material short-term goals, such as a new car or a promotion within a month or two; don't be afraid to list extremely idealistic or long-term goals, such as career-overview statements, health statements, or lifelong directives. Remember, you are instructing yourself to succeed, targeting goals you have chosen as harmonious with your belief system. By reciting your list faithfully, you will begin controlling and optimizing your reality map without having to microanalyze its shortcomings.

We recommend reconstructing the entire list whenever you realize that some entry is in the wrong position, because this indicates an emerging conflict between the root level of your belief-system tree and your reality map. Conflict of this sort creates an irresolute actor whose energy is spent fighting internal battles.

Using your targeting list, you can and must reconcile the differences between your reality map and the maps of others with whom you must interact. More, you can remain true to your belief system and substantially increase your competitive capability by focusing on the differences between you and your competitors and exploiting your relative strengths.

All behavior, business included, succeeds only to the extent that it is motivated by sound judgment. Products and services must fill a real need and perform creditably. If a supplier is cutting a logistical corner in haste to reach a goal—as happened prior to the *Challenger* explosion—his effort will ultimately fail. If a procurement officer cuts the same corner by contracting with just such a competitor, the procurer is underwriting eventual failure. Although money may change hands and benefits apparently accrue to individuals who provide substandard goods and services, in many cases their credibility and reputation eventually will suffer as a result—as increasing numbers of congressional and procurement scandals clearly demonstrate. Not in the short term, perhaps, but ultimately, in the larger time frame where the big ones are won and lost, morality counts.

What do we mean by morality? We mean your subjective and personal sense of right and wrong, developed in a context of cultural ethics. If you meet your own behavioral standard, your actions have a much greater chance of success, because the expectations of your reality map are consonant with your belief-system tree.

Warriors must know what they are fighting for and believe in it. People who act in accordance with their belief systems succeed, in part, because they feel they are right and thus deserve to succeed.

Your expectation—your reality map—acting in concert with your belief system focuses you in time. Your expectation is your time sense, explicitly setting time limits on your accomplishments while implicitly defining your feeling about time itself—whether you control time or time controls you. If you are more comfortable taking the short view, do so consciously, but remember that visionaries are those who have trained themselves to focus on the big picture.

Models of Reality

In the following chapters, we will unroll a reality map that includes telepathy, psychokinesis, and manipulation of time by the human mind. To perform extraordinary acts, some warriors need only faith. Others need to know that what they are doing is behavior accepted by authorities they respect.

Here is a quick and dirty survey of the theoretical reality maps used by many on the leading edge of physical thought in engineering, physics, and government to approach extraordinary phenomena in a rational context.

1. The electromagnetic (EM) model suggests that we are biological transceivers attuned to the psychic frequencies. This model is favored by Soviet and Eastern European scientists.[4] Here, geophysical wave processes such as geoseismic and infrasonic waves are considered potential carriers for human mind/body communications.

2. The anthropic model postulates that human minds shape the reality they observe, that we order the random processes of the universe with our consciousness.

3. The quantum-mechanical model suggests that the mind prefers recognizing static moments of "reality" but also interacts with wave phenomena on a continual basis. Thus, consciousness has access to the future and the past as well as the present.[5]

4. The holographic model suggests that human consciousness transforms frequency and amplitude information into intelligible sensory impressions.[6]

A Wider Reality

No one knows which, if any, of these models is the correct one. No one knows for certain how consciousness interacts with the phenomenal world. Bell's theorem (proving locality is incompatible with quantum-mechanical laws)[7] suggests that either we view the world as fundamentally interconnected or we imbue consciousness with the power to directly affect and connect reality.

Einstein's relativity offers us "frozen passage," in which all events are independently fixed and consciousness moves over them, from the past to the future, like a train on railroad tracks.

Governments around the world are interested in these models, because recent analyses of paranormal phenomena suggest that time itself may be open to manipulation. If we can acquire reliable information about future events and manipulate coincidence, the very conduct of warfare, espionage, and business will change dramatically. So will the global reality map.

The warrior needs the best reality map he can get. You may choose from among these potential reality maps, if you like, any model that delimits your perceptions of what is and is not possible. You may choose a reality map where ESP, psychokinesis, and mental access to events in the future are all possible. You may wish to call these events noncausal, nonlocal quantum effects. You may call them paranormal effects or psychic phenomena. But whatever you call them, the boundaries of your reality map are now broader than they were, and we can venture into this larger world.

6

A STILL SMALL VOICE: INTUITIVE DECISION MAKING

For time immemorial, warriors and their intuition have been inextricably linked. Battles, campaigns, even wars have been won or lost on the intuition of leaders—that inner knowledge providing great warriors with the edge to prevail over circumstances. The warrior bets his life on his intuitive decision making. You too can learn how to recognize intuition in action, when to go with your gut, and how to turn gut feelings into winning action.

The classic example of warrior intuition is the infantry point man. The point man in a patrol is the individual who goes first. He is in the greatest danger, for he will encounter the enemy first as his unit moves forward to make contact. He must spot potential ambushes, mine fields, and other booby traps. His life is undeniably on the line; the lives of the men in his unit are in his hands.

Old infantry hands will tell you: Never put a "dud" on the point. In Vietnam, where point duty was often used by inexperienced leaders as punishment for screwing up, the results are history. In war fighting, it is a truism that certain people possess intangible qualities that make them good point men. In units that rotate everyone through the point position, point men suffer extremely high casualties.

Successful point men have the *intuition* that leads their patrol safely through great danger. They simply "feel" where ambushes are. They sense danger lurking in the bush. They know when to stop, proceed, or run. This sixth sense is renowned throughout the combat arms of fighting forces around the world.

In Vietnam, John Alexander commanded a Special Forces A-Team operating in the Mekong Delta area known as the Seven Mountains. The mountains were a stronghold first for the Viet Cong and later for the NVA. Leading a small patrol deep into Viet Cong turf, Alexander felt a sudden need to stop, as if his men were likely to encounter the enemy. Something just didn't seem right. Slowly, he began backing up, then abruptly stopped in midstride. Alexander knew there was no logical reason to stop; in fact, all indications pointed to the patrol's rapidly evacuating the area.

Looking down, Alexander saw, across the back of his boot, a booby trap's trip wire, already taut, pulling on the pin of a hand grenade less than two feet from his legs. If he'd moved another two or three inches, the grenade could have blown off his legs. That inner knowing—the *sensing* that stopped him for no apparent reason to check his surroundings—probably saved his life.

Throughout his tour in Vietnam, including the infamous Tet offensive of 1968, Alexander's intuition helped his combat-operations team run some of the most dangerous missions in the Mekong Delta. No American was ever killed under his command. Six weeks after Alexander left Vietnam, his replacement was killed in an explosion in his own camp.

In 1983, when Alexander was giving a briefing to Lieutenant General Robert Kingston (then commander of U.S. Forces Central Command (CENTCOM) at MacDill Air Force Base, Florida), Kingston told of similar incidents in Vietnam. He would have an urge to move to another location and find, when he had, that where he'd been standing moments before was now an artillery or mortar strike zone.

Great combat leaders, such as General George Patton, while leading people fearlessly into combat, often appear to be doing illogical things, such as exposing themselves to enemy fire. History equates this with extreme bravery, but such individuals frequently remark that they "just knew" nothing would happen to them; at times when they knew intuitively that they were in danger, they were injured.

There have been many cases of soldiers who handed their comrades a letter, saying, "This is my last battle; be sure my wife gets this." As well as literature on combat fatalities, a body of evidence exists indicating that people "know," at least unconsciously, when they are about to die. Dr. Elisabeth Kübler-Ross suggests that *all* people know this at some level, and uses a process of interpretive drawings to prove this point. [1]

Kübler-Ross tells of a young girl who was playing near an ocean beach. For several days, her mother wouldn't allow her to go into the water with the other children. Finally, the girl went out into the water and was attacked by a shark, rare in that area. Among the little girl's possessions were found three pictures she'd drawn at the beach. The first showed a girl swimming on top of the water. The second depicted a girl on a raft with a shark swimming by. The third fateful drawing placed the girl in the shark's mouth under the water.

PROGRESS AND INTUITION

Reliance on intuition runs contrary to contemporary fashion. Many scientists and business analysts would like everything reduced to an equation and entered into a computer, so that when all the numbers are properly crunched, the right answer is unfailingly displayed. This is the basic rationale behind artificial intelligence (AI) and expert systems.

Despite promises of quick payback from research in artificial intelligence, some elements of the scientific community are now backing away from earlier claims. Artificial intelligence today is made up of expert-system shells that are either rule based or example based. Both types of shells are predicated on long chains of "if . . . then" questions, answered at each step by either yes or no. This treatment of the "real" world as a step function (i.e., all responses are either black or white), while labeled intelligent, is limited in scope and fails to incorporate the subtle cognitive/intuitive processes of human thought.

We are entering a period of continually greater reliance on expert systems and computer programs to determine trends, predict the future and tell us what we see. Most of us remember the chaos on Black Monday, Oct. 13, 1987, when programmed computer trading ran wild and the stock market plummeted. Man must be left "in the loop." In many areas, where information-handling systems are oversaturated with critical data, problems stem from the lack of bold, well-trained, intuitive human analysts.

In today's technical-intelligence collections systems, one of the military's chief concerns is how to prevent overloading commanders with too much information. Although data fusion is touted as a panacea, data overload can be just as damaging to the decision-making process as data insufficiency.

Combat represents a worst-case scenario for decision making. In combat, the warrior is making life-and-death decisions with limited information. Recent impact studies on electronic-battlefield technology indicate the increasing importance of improved reconnaissance sensor platforms and surveillance-and-target-acquisition systems, as well as command, control, communications, and intelligence (or C3I) systems. With advanced technology, the commander may have more information but never all the information necessary. Command must still rely on intuitive decision making.

The Israelis recognize this fact. While we use the acronym C3I to discuss our battlefield command parameters, they speak of I3L: intuition, intelligence, improvisation, and luck. According to the Israelis, this is what *really* occurs in the decision loop on the field of battle.

EUREKA

Science still depends on the intuitive flashes that lead to dramatic breakthroughs. This process of discovery is called the "Eureka effect," from a story about Archimedes, the Greek scientist.

Archimedes, on orders from King Hiero II of Syracuse, was trying to determine the amount of gold in a crown without melting it down. Relaxing in a hot bath, watching the tub overflow, he suddenly realized that the displacement of water made by gold (an extremely dense metal) should be less than the displacement of water made by gold mixed with an alloy. Excited by his discovery of the Archimedes principle, he ran, naked and wet, down the streets yelling, "Eureka!"—literally, "I have found it."

The Eureka effect has historically occurred during relaxation after intense study. Most frequently, those who have these insights have been working their problem for some time and are letting go when insight comes to them.

Einstein reported that his thinking began with images he could then merge. Dr. Jonas Salk, inventor of the Salk polio vaccine, was noted for listening to his internal self-talk.

This process appears to be out of favor in the modern age as we spend more time on evolutionary progression and product improvement and less on basic science. Scientific trends are following three distinct technological paths: evolutionary, revolutionary, and radical.

Evolutionary technologies evolve from current growth trends in science, working systems or technologies under research and development. Developments in these areas could include a manned lunar colony, lightweight tactical body armor, or inexpensive commercial robotics.

Revolutionary technologies come from fundamental research.

Areas of great potential include superconductivity, genetic engineering, macroscopic weather engineering, and psychotronics.

Radical technologies are those that change the global reality map. Such children of the Eureka effect could come from basic theoretical research into time travel, controllable nonlocal quantum effects, or virtual-state engineering. Whatever the next such breakthrough may be, you can be sure it will be a product of intuition.

Dr. Arthur J. Deikman, writing for *New Realities*, suggested that "intuition is a process that is fundamentally different from, and superior to, reason, in discovering truth."[2] The Nobel prize-winning physicist Eugene Wigner said: "The discovery of the laws of nature requires first and foremost intuition, conceiving of pictures and a great many subconscious processes. The use and also the confirmation of these laws is another matter . . . logic comes after intuition."[3] And the great mathematician Carl Friedrich Gauss stated, "I have had my solutions for a long time, but I do not yet know how I am to arrive at them."[4]

Defining what intuition is can be quite difficult. Philip Goldberg, author of *The Intuitive Edge*,[5] defines intuition mainly in terms of what it is not. Andrew Weil, in his book *The Natural Mind*,[6] states, "Intuitive flashes are transient, spontaneous altered states of consciousness consisting of particular sensory experience or thoughts, coupled with strong emotional reactions," and suggests that intuition is an internal process of rational or analytic thought.

Some psychologists argue that intuition, rather than being a supernatural or an unconscious process, is subliminally provided perception of data or insight already available to unconscious cueing. Rather than choose from among these explanations, we recommend that you temporarily set aside belief systems, apply the process we will describe and, if it works, continue to use it at your discretion.

Everyone has experienced intuitive insights. Many respond to them; others deny and repress them. Buckminster Fuller, creator of the geodesic dome, called the intuitive process cosmic fishing: "Once you feel a nibble, you've got to hook the fish."[7] Too often, people do not capitalize on their inspirations.

Intuitive insights come in many forms. To some, these flashes occur as images; to others, intuition comes as verbal input; still others report a general sense of "knowing."

Silvano Arieti, in his book *Creativity: The Magic Synthesis*,[8] postulates that preconscious thoughts may spark creativity or intuitive insight. He suggests that we transform these intuitions into visions, images, or words, so that they can be verbalized and acted upon.

Abraham Maslow, in *The Farther Reaches of Human Nature*,[9] proposed that during moments of creativity, it becomes impossible to differentiate between self and not self. Maslow contends that people who have emphasized self-development are better equipped to apply their intuitive skills.

DEVELOPING THE IDM PROCESS

To develop the IDM (intuitive decision making) process, we will build on the skills already learned in earlier chapters. Negativity can impact one's ability to perceive personal intuitive processes. We ask that you now temporarily set aside the doubt in your belief system and try this process:

First, quiet the mind. Next, define the problem you wish to solve. Now, identify what is unique to the problem, and look for gaps in your knowledge. The IDM process works to connect diverse and sometimes abstract pieces of data, creating a pattern out of discrete bits by giving a nonlinear function a cognitive path.

While working on a complex problem, carry a small pad of paper and jot down ideas as they come to you. Innovative solutions tend to pop into our heads at unexpected times, as if the mind collates complex data best while our attention is distracted. Allow some time each day to let your mind wander, without focusing on a specific issue. Often these intuitive flashes occur while traveling, especially for long distances, or while playing sports or exercising. Many good ideas come right before sleep; make sure to write those down or you may not remember in the morning.

To apply modeling techniques to the IDM process, use yourself as the expert to be modeled. Remember when you made a correct decision based on intuition rather than analysis. Also consider decisions where both factors were involved. Recall how you felt internally. What was your physical and emotional state? Do you remember any changes in physiology? Try to recreate the feeling you got when you knew you had the right answer.

Once you've re-created the state, anchor it physically and try working from that state when you next need a creative response. Remember that in the Jedi Project, the last step the experts took was a kinesthetic check: Their final decision to shoot came from an internal, intuitive feeling that things were right. Find that feeling in yourself, and you've modeled the IDM process as you can best utilize it.

Key to the IDM process is using educated guesses in conjunction with intuition—fusing intuition with analysis. IDM should be employed as part of the decision-making process of the independent thinker.

The American military has a history of independence. It is considered an American trait the world over. Intuition on the battlefield means the difference between life and death. Guessing when or where to move, intuiting where there is danger, is an ability crucial to individual and group survival in the field.

All our most sophisticated electronic-sensor systems can only provide us with data on troop disposition; none gets inside the heads of the enemy leadership and provides information on the enemy's intent.

It is axiomatic in intelligence that intent is the hardest call to make. Intuition often calls enemy intent correctly. The field commander knows this. The intuitive commander knows what the enemy will do and, frequently, when that enemy will do it.

FEAR OF FAILURE AS A LEARNING TOOL

Fear of failure can impact intuition. Positive use of the fear of failure was developed by former Apollo astronaut Edgar Mitchell. Mitchell, a retired naval officer with a Ph.D. from MIT, founded the Institute of Noetic Sciences, an organization dedicated to the development of IDM capabilities and their applications in the business world.

Mitchell fervently believes that the ability to rely on the intuitive response is the most critical part of an astronaut's training. "We spent ten percent of our time studying plans for the mission and ninety percent learning how to react intuitively to all the 'what ifs.' "[10]

Mitchell is an advocate of failure analysis, a discipline born of the U.S. space program and used to define and determine the weakest link in any chain of complex processes. By carefully interviewing key workers, seasoned foremen, and front-line production managers, executives can draw on their experiences and gut-level fears and doubts about where Murphy's Law will impact a production process.

In Mitchell's words: "With a computer printout of the resulting 'fault tree' in front of him, a boss can almost smell those failures before they occur."[11]

GOING AGAINST THE TIDE

Many advances in science and technology have resulted from free thinkers, who either break or temporarily suspend the rules of the game.

Innovations are often made by people who change careers during middle age. This phenomenon is called the novice effect. Louis Pasteur and Francis Crick are just two examples of pioneers who changed careers in midstream and made innovative mental connections in their new fields of study.

The novice effect is one way to continue expanding intellectual growth. Some experts counsel people to abandon their area of expertise every few years and explore "a new problem or one that is fascinating but about which they are totally ignorant. Subjected to a novel barrage of experiences, the brain is forced to grow, to make new neural connections, to see the world with fresh eyes."[12]

The creation of this book is a case in point. The new challenges facing each of the authors were consciously sought precisely because the novice effect can lead to such exciting results and deep personal satisfaction.

Yet the decision to come together to do this project was made intuitively—a series of snap judgments based on a "feeling" experienced by all concerned that such a joint venture would prove rewarding.

Intuitive decision making on a consensus basis is one of the specialties of the Moebius Group, a think tank run by Stephan Schwartz, a former special assistant to the chief of naval operations.[13] In Los Angeles, California, Schwartz uses groups of intuitives to investigate paranormal phenomena. The Moebius Group is the only for-profit organization employing advanced human technologies (such as remote viewing) in a business environment.

Schwartz employs intuitively gathered data as well as traditional analysis and claims statistically significant results on hard business calls such as the stock market.

The Center for Applied Intuition uses a similar approach to tackle difficult scientific and technical problems.

The Soviets employ related techniques in their approach to psychotronic and parapsychological research.

The intuitive process does not work in a vacuum. Using internal, sometimes subconscious, knowledge of facts, data points, and/or sensory impressions, it can provide a coherent picture where none is available by other means.

The warrior needs his intuition. We hope we have convinced you that you need yours.

7

AS FAR AS THE MIND CAN SEE: VISUALIZATION

From the field station to the strategy room under the White House, the ability to visualize what may and can occur is crucial. Intelligence professionals speak of anticipation as a trainable skill, comprised of information, intuition, and visualization, that helps its practitioners prepare for the enemy's moves before he makes them.

During the revolt of the Chinese students in Tiananmen Square, the world media waxed euphoric, believing that under its watchful eye, the Chinese leadership could do nothing but accede to the students' demands for freedom.

The intelligence community had another vision. Dr. Ray S. Cline, former deputy director of CIA and an old China hand, remarked to Janet Morris on the phone during those days that no matter how many media interviews he did, Dr. Cline couldn't seem to make people "see" what he "knew" so clearly: The Chinese government would crush the students, no matter how much blood was shed.

All through the intelligence community during that interval, the debate was about how and when, not if, the government of China would move. Two days before the tanks began to roll,

Janet Morris and friends were discussing the possible response of the Chinese government. No one doubted that military action was imminent; the debate was over what form it would take.

One of those present spoke of Chinese tanks in Tiananmen Square as if it had already happened. Others suggested that air power would be a cleaner, more likely response, but this man was adamant: It would be tanks that crushed the students. When pressed to support his certainty with reason, he responded that the Chinese gerontocracy would use the same tactics that brought them to power—infantry tactics. But his anticipation was clearly based on more than that. He believed that he already "saw" the situation played out correctly.

At the highest levels of command, the warrior must be able to visualize what *can be*. A commander must visualize the objective; conceptualize the battle before opposing forces engage; then see the battle when in progress, in order to reevaluate strategy and add time-sensitive new decisions to the loop.

Visualization of the desired objective is the most critical of these components. The commander must have the ability to mentally picture how best to employ available forces, predict the reaction of enemy forces, and formulate a way in which his actions can lead to success on the battlefield.

Once the battle has commenced, there is the additional requirement of relaying new information to his field officers in near-real time so that the battle in progress may be course corrected by timely decisions.

All of these activities must occur in the mind of the commander. The successful commander has trained himself to mentally visualize and manipulate these images by playing out competing scenarios. This includes visualizing the desired objective before the battle starts. The final outcome of the battle will depend on the commander's ability to conceptualize how the event will take place, his decisions as to when and where to commit his forces, and his ability to guide the unfolding battle through newly gathered intelligence.

This need to visualize applies at every level, from the individual mosquito-wing soldier on the battlefield to corps commanders fighting the operational level of war. And let us not forget the service chiefs, the secretariat, and even the commander-in-chief, charged with the strategic defense of the United States. All must possess this ability to visualize the outcome, imperative to the national defense at all levels.

This ability can be nurtured and developed for use in the warfare of everyday life.

THE STEPS IN THE PROCESS

Visualization provides us with a new way of seeing problems, thereby increasing our chances for successful solution. It also provides us with a tool for "increasing our ability to remember, by associating nonvisual information with visual cues, and, perhaps, more important, enabling us to vividly rehearse or experience events mentally."[1]

In sports, the ability to visualize has long been recognized as one of the imperative factors for producing excellence. Many athletes use visualization to "see" themselves performing their skill with winning perfection—before they enter into competition.

We mentioned earlier how experts improved their pistol-shooting scores after participating in the Jedi Project. One man who significantly increased his score following the modeling intervention was the national champion, whose performance had fallen off slightly. Initially, he had mentally shot the entire match the day prior to the actual competition. He would sit down and then, quietly, in his mind, review *everything* in sequence, from the time he arrived and placed his gun on the stand until he'd fire every single shot of the match, rehearsing the entire match from start to finish. This shooter kept a souvenir target to help with his visualization—one that he had scored particularly well with; ten shots in the Ten-X range, all in the center of the bull's eye. He kept the target inside his gun case. Before each match, he could look at this example of what he had been visualizing in his mind: a perfect score. After he won the championship, he became cocky and discontinued these practices.

During the Jedi Project, the shooter realized the value of the visualization techniques he once had used faithfully. He reinstated them in his preparation ritual. A short time after participating in the Jedi Project, he wrote a letter from Fort Benning, indicating that his score had now gone up the ten or so points he'd been missing during his slump. He was back in winning form again, which he attributed directly to the reinstatement of his visualization techniques.

To visualize task accomplishment in its most complete form, a virtual blueprint of perfection is necessary. Visualize the task *as if it has already been done*. It is this component of *completion*, of mentally putting the event in the past tense, that seems to be crucial to task perfection. The experts who use this technique do not describe what they are *going* to do; they describe the task as being successfully and perfectly completed.

When visualizing the task, the experts do so in as complete detail as possible. They include every aspect: seeing it, hearing it, and/or feeling it. They add every detail, no matter how small, until they do it to perfection. You should too.

To enhance your capabilities through visualization, you must:

1. Know your objective and be able to visualize it.

2. See the act being accomplished in complete detail and in perfect form.

3. Internalize the act as though you have already accomplished it.

You can apply this technique to any skill you desire to master. In sports, there are two useful types of visualization training. The first type is enhanced physical vision.

Three elements are normally associated with physical vision training. First is basic visual training: keeping the individual's head still while increasing tracking and visual accommodation capabilities. Second is advanced visual training. This includes rapid presentation of objects, plus some fundamentals of mental imagery. The final part is the enhancement program, accom-

As Far as the Mind Can See: Visualization

plished through sensory overload. During sensory overload, a large number of visual signals are presented in a changing environment to which the trainee must adapt quickly.

Such training can be used by air-traffic controllers, pilots, or in sports involving quick reactions to a large number of simultaneously occurring visual sensory cues.

Physical vision training can benefit anyone who drives a car in congested traffic patterns or who plays sports. The training program described above is a formal program, requiring special equipment. However, there are simple ways to improve your vision skills.

To try the following exercise, enlist a friend. Pick a spot directly in front of you. Keeping your eyes pointed toward that spot, note how much you can see peripherally. Extend your arms in front of you. Move your arms horizontally to your side. Note when they pass out of sight. Wiggle your fingers to be sure you see them. With normal vision, you should be able to see 180 degrees or more.

Now have your friend move to one side of you and hold up some fingers. Look straight ahead. Count the fingers. Have your friend move slowly behind you, until out of your field of view.

Or try watching television at an increasing angle to the set. Don't focus in front of you; expand your field to include a wider area. Sentries are taught not to stare at objects at night because such objects apparently move or disappear. This is due to the construction of the human eye. By looking to the right or left, it's easier to tell what's where. On patrol, if you focus on your immediate path, you may not notice danger to one side.

To increase visual accommodation of rapidly changing scenes or stimuli, flick your TV set quickly from station to station. Note the amount of detail you can discern on each channel. Practice, and try to improve your performance. Pilots in combat must keep track of their location in relation to the ground, other aircraft (friendly and hostile), and the position of ground forces. You may use this to improve your tennis, computer gaming, or to track drivers on the highway.

THE POWER OF PREVISUALIZATION

The beauty of previsualization is that it is not limited to activities of short duration but can be applied to complex and protracted situations, with no ceiling on the number of variables.

Previsualization can be used to aid or create muscle memory. Muscle memory is the body's way of learning and remembering physical tasks. It played an important part in the expert-shooting exercise. When operating under extreme conditions, one has no time to think out each step of an action independently. Muscle memory contains the body's stored knowledge of a previous proper performance of some task. When you call upon muscle memory, your body automatically conducts the same routine. Previsualization is used by professional athletes to help reinforce that muscle memory.

During the 1984 Winter Olympic trials, Bob Said, a former Grand Prix racing champion and leader of two Olympic and five U.S. World bobsled teams, commented on the merits of previsualization and its effect on muscle memory: "In the sled, you know where you want to be in each corner, so that when you get into the corner, you're already programmed for coming out. . . . If you have to *think* a reaction to the sled, even if you have the world's fastest reactions, you're too slow. . . . It's not a sharpening of the abilities so much as it's allowing one's abilities to function as they're supposed to. . . ."[2]

Properly directed thought can have tremendous impact on the world of action. We are increasingly incorporating mental imagery in the treatment of disease. Many cases have been cited of individuals using visualization techniques to reduce cancer in "guided-imagery" treatment programs at prestigious hospitals, such as the Yale University medical center. Patients may be asked to picture their cancer and then mentally marshal an army of white cells to attack and eliminate it. Children may mentally picture warriors, gunships, or death rays attacking and destroying the cancer.

A number of doctors, including Elisabeth Kübler-Ross,

As Far as the Mind Can See: Visualization

Bernie Siegel, and Carl and Stephanie Simonton, have all been quite successful with patients applying this technique.

To enhance internal visualization, patients actually draw on paper pictures of their disease and its cure. The important factor for the individual is belief that the visualized events are really occurring.

The power of imagery may blur the line between fantasy and reality and may play a part in psychosomatic diseases. The mind's image of health or illness may be more powerful than we currently believe.

There is a downside to visualization. These physical and mental effects can be negative as well as positive. One area where the most serious consequences of negative imagery can be seen is in the medical community. The doctor/patient relationship is emotionally charged, and fertile ground for the implantation of powerful images in the minds of the suggestible.

Dr. Siegel and others suggest that a doctor who describes a patient with a heart condition as "a walking time bomb" or who gives a patient "three months to live" may unwittingly be implanting physiology-altering images and sentencing that patient to death by self-fulfilling prophecy.

Dr. Martin L. Rossman, who uses imagery in his medical practice, considers worry to be one of the most common forms of debilitative imagery: "Worry creates negative images of some future event like a deadline or a test. The downside is that chronic worry can overwork and wear down the immune system, leading to chronic stress, a state that has been associated with numerous ailments, from headaches to heart disease. The upside is that people who develop psychosomatic symptoms also have the greatest success in using imagery to resolve them."[3]

Medical practitioners use two categories of imagery: receptive imagery and active imagery.

Receptive imagery, a *diagnostic* tool, uses relaxation techniques and biofeedback to generate images and discussions leading to the cause of the patient's symptoms. This process alone can rid the patient of symptoms, provided their basis is psychosomatic.[4]

Active imagery is a *treatment* tool, divided in two general categories: process imagery and end-state imagery. "In process imagery, one works with symbolic images of the actual physiological processes that are needed to heal. In end state, one imagines freedom from symptoms and a return to the favored activities allowed by good health."[5]

Active imagery is an adjunct to such treatments as radiation or chemotherapy, and assists in preparation for other medical procedures. Dr. Errol Korn, director of the Scripps Memorial Hospital Pain Rehabilitation Center, cites numerous studies in which imagery "seemed to produce a variety of positive outcomes, including reduced blood loss during surgery, faster wound healing, shortened hospital stays, and reduced drug requirements."[6]

The National Research Council's panel on Enhancing Human Performance, who reviewed visualization techniques, recognized the requirement for additional research in the area.[7]

The U.S. Army medical establishment has been using visualization techniques for several years. In 1983, Rich Groller, the victim of esophageal spasms, spent a week in the cardiac-care unit of the Letterman U.S. Army Medical Center in San Francisco. Subsequent to diagnosis, Groller was taught guided-imagery relaxation techniques, which the medical staff routinely administers for relaxation therapy and stress management.

John Alexander participated in a meeting with Secretary of the Army John Marsh during which the positive potential of visualization was discussed and the secretary suggested it warranted further research. During this discussion, Soviet advances in visualization were also discussed, with particular attention paid to the Soviets' use of previsualization as a training methodology for combat-skill enhancement.

ENHANCING MENTAL IMAGERY: THE SUCCESS SPACE
Everyone has the ability to visualize. We need only to develop
these skills.

First, read this exercise. Then have someone read it to you
while you follow the instructions:

To begin enhancing your ability to visualize, find a comfortable position, preferably sitting upright.

Close your eyes and breathe deeply.

You are now relaxing and becoming more mentally alert.

Envision an object, something familiar to you: a baseball, a
rose, an orange. The object is floating before you, against a
neutral background. Choose a background color and envision
the object of your choice floating between you and that colored
background.

Now bring your object closer. Magnify it. How does it look
close up? Magnify it again. See the internal structure of the
object, the molecules composing it.

Return the object to normal size. See it floating against your
colored background. Now turn the object. How does it look from
the back? From the underside? From above?

Move the object toward your background color, farther
and farther, until it is just a dot. Bring it toward you very fast.
Stop the object at a comfortable distance. Write your name on
it in a contrasting color. Put it away for later use. Anytime you
wish, you may bring it back and use it for any purpose you
desire.

Now you have only the background color before your eyes, an
expanse of the color of your choice. On this background, you
have just proved to yourself that you can project any item you
desire. You can manipulate that item in space. You can get
inside it and see its internal structure.

This background color is your key color. Against this colored background, you can visualize and manipulate any objects, persons, places, or things you choose. Whenever you

call up this colored expanse, you are in control of whatever you bring before you.

You can use this background to practice sports, muscle memory, any skill you desire.

To prove this to yourself, create a basketball court with walls of your background color. Create a shooting range. Create a problem-solving room just for you, where you can go anytime and access all the skills you have learned and will learn, in complete privacy and with positive results.

This is your success space. Once you have claimed this space, you can use it to enhance your performance in any area of human endeavor. If you wish, create a video screen in your space on which you can view information. Add a sound system if you like, so that you can hear information if the need arises.

You can go to your success space for visualization, for meditation, for problem solving, for relaxation and health benefits at any time, simply by closing your eyes, taking a deep breath, and visualizing the color you have chosen.

Once your friend has read you the exercise and you have completed the steps, you may want to read it to your friend. The success-space visualization exercise is a problem-solving tool that sets no limits on possibility. Using this technique, solutions may occur to you that are symbolic, or they may be real-time solutions that you can implement immediately.

Albert Einstein reported using mental imagery to solve problems. Einstein's formulation of the theory of relativity sprang from the idea of mentally riding a beam of light backward to its source. So thoroughly was Einstein using visualization techniques for problem solving that he visualized himself facing the source of the light beam as he rode in order to "see" where it came from.

Using the visualization technique above, why not take a ride on a light beam and see what Einstein saw?

GOAL SETTING

James Fadiman, Ph.D., a psychologist and noted teacher, is quoted as saying, "It is awesome how easily people's lives change when they set goals." The next step in creative visualization is to establish goals. Although individual goals are specific, workable goals will never be at odds with the person's reality map, which must support them. As the saying goes, be careful what you wish for. This is a potent technique and one that, if not under conscious control, can cause difficulties because the subconscious may be setting goals for you.

For most successful people, setting goals is a matter of routine. Many military and business organizations use a technique called strategic planning. Properly executed, strategic planning is a version of corporate goal setting, where corporate leaders meet and jointly establish the company's goals for the short, mid, and long term. No company executive could afford to respond, when asked what he wanted to do next, by saying, "I don't know."

Neither can anyone involved with creative visualization. Like an organization, a successful individual cannot afford to proceed without an orderly pattern, drifting along and hoping for the best. In the action services, it's said, "Act, don't react."

Goal setting tends to be an intimate process. How intimate? Janet Morris, at a crucial moment in her career, needed a mentor in Washington, someone high in the analytical community. She researched the possible candidates and chose Dr. Ray S. Cline, former assistant secretary of state and deputy director of CIA. Since she knew no one close to Dr. Cline, she attended a seminar where he was speaking. Dr. Cline and Janet Morris are currently working together on a book.

John Alexander says, "When I first joined the Army, in basic training I took a turn at guard duty. During that first night, I saw an officer wearing both Airborne jump wings and a Ranger tab. At that moment, I decided I wanted to be an Airborne Ranger officer. It took years, but I made that vision a reality."

How? Learn what you really want. Use the targeting list already described if you're not sure what your goals are—or should be. Once you've established your list, evaluate it. Now, take the items on your list and focus the goals into images. Next, use your success-space and creative-visualization techniques to energize the images of yourself happily having achieved your goals.

The warrior needs to visualize the outcome of a battle, to see and understand the situation as combat progresses. The advanced warrior knows the advantage that previsualization gives in the acquisition of physical skills. The warrior recognizes the value of using visualization to realize goals. The tools are available; you need only to use them.

8

AND NOTHING WILL BE HIDDEN FROM YOU: REMOTE VIEWING

Billions of dollars are spent each year by the world's nations to research, develop, and procure remote-sensing systems. Orbiting spy satellites now monitor vast expanses of the globe, targeted on foreign soil. Yet even the most sophisticated remote-sensing platform cannot provide all the data required to understand an adversary's intentions.

Since the beginnings of armed conflict, commanders have yearned for more and better information on the location, disposition, and intent of enemy forces. Traditionally, any source is a good source as long as it provides reliable information about the enemy. Spy planes, listening stations, and satellites are relatively new additions to the arsenals of the world's intelligence communities.

Throughout recorded history, leaders have attempted to use psychics to predict the behavior of warlike enemies. Court astrologers arose with Babylon. The ancient Greeks used a series of female oracles who spoke from sites such as Delphi.

That tradition continues today. According to *U.S. News and World Report*, "As far as back as 1981, intelligence agents from the Pentagon relied on psychics, first to help determine the whereabouts of a kidnapped U.S. general, and later to locate the Beirut headquarters of an Iran-backed Hezbollah organization, believed to be the keepers of the U.S. hostages."[1]

Until recently, governments relied on innately talented individuals to provide such information. Those gifted people—such psi stars as Uri Geller and the Soviet psychics Kulagina, Vinogradova, and Ermolayev—had reputations that rose and fell based on single performances. Commanders, with only individual results and reputations to go by, were forced to trust their own personal intuition regarding the reliability of the information they received.

The Pentagon reportedly sent half a dozen psychics to Italy to help the Italians find the captured American general James Lee Dozier. The Italians treated this information very seriously.[2] Whether the counterintelligence effort that rescued Dozier was actually aided by the information of American psychics remains a matter of debate. But psychic function, always of interest to governments, is now being studied scientifically in laboratories around the world.

Remote viewing is the technical term for a specific psychic information-gathering process. Remote viewing is the ability of an individual to mentally acquire information about objects or events at a distance—whether those objects or events exist in the past, present, or future.

Remote viewers gather information as effectively from the future or the past as they do from the present. This has an obvious allure for government policy makers and business entrepreneurs.

Sometimes a remote viewer gathers his information by contacting an observer at the designated site during the chosen interval. In other cases, the remote viewer gathers information without contacting an observer at the target location.

The first major research institution to study remote viewing was Stanford Research Institute, or SRI International. There, Dr. Hal Puthoff and Mr. Russell Targ conducted a series of experiments using such "stars" as Pat Price, Ingo Swann, and

Hella Hammid. The results were impressive, and they made a good first attempt to do scientifically valid experiments.

Their studies indicated that information could indeed be extracted by a remote viewer at a distance from a target site. The remote viewer did not have to know the identity of the target or be told any specifics about its nature.[3]

Studies continue. Major contributions to the field are being provided by Dr. Robert Jahn and Ms. Brenda Dunne of Princeton University. Dr. Jahn established the Princeton Engineering Anomalies Laboratory to study scientifically the effect of consciousness on the external world.

Jahn and Dunne, using rigorous experimental techniques, avoided the methodological flaws that had plagued earlier studies and brought down the wrath of the scientific community. They are still collecting quantifiable results suggesting that the mental signals being transmitted by one subject and received by another subject contain more information than chance predicts. In their experiments, descriptions of specific targets removed from the subject in time and space consistently prove more accurate than chance guesses about the specifics of unknown targets could be.

In Menlo Park, California, at SRI, the first definitive experiments of this sort were conducted. These early experiments involved three participants: an experimenter; a remote viewer, or subject; and an on-site observer. The on-site observer went to a designated site and looked at the target while the remote viewer sat in the lab at SRI, being watched by the experimenter, and wrote down impressions of what the on-site observer was seeing at that time.

Each target was chosen randomly from an established target pool of distinctive sites close to SRI. The actual site used in any experiment was chosen by the on-site observer by throwing dice once the observer was in a car. That way, the experimenter did not know which site had been chosen until the experiment was over. Thus, the experimenter couldn't unintentionally cue the remote viewer.

Pedestrian Overpass Target

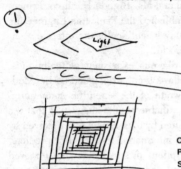

Subject Hammid drawing, described as "some kind of diagonal trough up in the air"

COURTESY OF H. E. PUTHOFF, PH.D., INSTITUTE FOR ADVANCED STUDIES, AUSTIN, TEXAS.

In example 1, the drawings and words relate to an overpass near Menlo Park. The remote viewer was Hella Hammid, who was sitting in the SRI research offices of Puthoff and Targ. She described the target as "some kind of diagonal trough up in the air."[4]

The early studies at SRI involved relatively short distances. The targets chosen were in the general vicinity of the laboratory, where they could be quickly reached and viewed. Eventually, experimenters decided to attempt to locate targets at greater and greater distances. Experiments have now been run intercontinentally. From these experiments, it appears that distance does not have any effect on the ability of an individual to locate and view a target.

In example 2, we have an intercontinental example from the Princeton studies of Jahn and Dunne. The target site was in Bratislava, Czechoslovakia; the viewer was in Wisconsin. This is a distance of approximately 5,600 miles, and yet, as the following text demonstrates, clearly accurate information was perceived: "I have the feeling that [the on-site observer] is somewhere near water. There might be boats. Several vertical lines, sort of like poles. They're narrow, not heavy. Maybe lampposts or flag poles. Some kind of circular shape. Almost like a merry-go-round or a gazebo. A large round thing. It's round on its side, like a disc, it's like a round thing flat on the ground, but it seems to have height as well. Maybe with poles. Could possibly come to a point on top. Sensing vertical lines again. Seems to be a strong impression, these vertical lines. No idea what they could be. . . . A definite sensation of being outside rather than in. Water again. . . . To one side of where [the on-site observer] is I get the feeling there's a kind of small building. Could be a shed. . . . Predominant colors seem to be blue and green. . . . Water again. Some very quick impression of a fence, a low fence. . . . Steps. I don't know where they're leading to. . . . The steps sort of lead up to like a path or walkway. Like a boardwalk. And there's a fence along it. There's people walking along it, and there's vertical lines along that walkway. . . ."[5]

In the Princeton experiment, when the remote viewer in Wisconsin was describing the Bratislava site, the on-site observer was *still* en route to the target location in Czechoslovakia. The remote-viewing experiment took place almost twenty-four hours *prior* to the time the observer in Czechoslovakia arrived at the target location. The viewer tried to describe what the observer *would see* after arriving on site.

Even more amazing than the great distances involved was that such remote-viewing events were not time dependent: Whether the target event was in the past, present, or future of the person trying to perceive them from a remote location had no bearing on the success of any given experiment. Remote-viewing experiments could produce equally valid data about past, present, or future events at the viewed locations. This led to a series of Princeton experiments, later confirmed by others, which dem-

DANUBE RIVER, BRATISLAVA, CZECHOSLOVAKIA—REMOTE PERCEPTION TARGET PHOTOS FIRST APPEARED IN *MARGINS OF REALITY* BY ROBERT JAHN, PH.D., AND BRENDA J. DUNNE.

And Nothing Will Be Hidden from You: Remote Viewing

onstrated that targets could be consistently viewed *precognitively:* The remote viewer could see, before the observer arrived at the target, what the observer would see, when on site.

It is this apparent ability of the human remote viewer to gather information from sites removed not only in space but in time that interests physicists. Because these results are qualitatively repeatable, they can be studied scientifically. To date, no attempt to model the physics of such data transfer has been wholly successful. Nevertheless, it appears that data is successfully being transferred from on-site observers to remote viewers.

Soviet work on remote viewing has attempted to explain the phenomenon as transmissions, by the human brain, of extreme low frequency (ELF) waves. Much Soviet work on remote perception is based on electromagnetic models.

After Russell Targ visited the Soviet Union at the invitation of the Soviet Academy of Science, he reported that some Soviet scientists had also found their subjects able to report information about a site before the site was chosen—precognitively "guess" the site to be chosen and describe it. The Soviet ELF model requires the target to be concurrently viewed by the remote viewer for real-time-data transfer to occur. No electromagnetic model of this process advanced so far allows for temporal distortion.[6]

Back in the U.S., Stephan Schwartz of the Moebius Group, in an experiment called Deep Quest, put remote viewers in submersible craft and asked them to view targets on land from a substantial underwater depth. That the viewers were successful, even though they were in a chamber shielded by water, suggests that the process at work is not electromagnetic in origin.[7] Schwartz proceeded to try psychically-assisted archaeology projects.[8] In triple-blind experiments, Schwartz attempted to pinpoint previously undiscovered sites, subsurface geology, and buried remains. Subsequent digs by the group discovered a buried city, though there was no way for the sensitives who'd worked on the project to have information about a target completely unexcavated previously.

PARTICIPATING IN REMOTE VIEWING

Several established methods, or protocols, exist for remote viewing. Literature by Jahn and Dunne,[9] by Puthoff and Targ,[10] Targ and Harary,[11] Jack Houck,[12] and even Ingo Swann,[13] all give instructions. Here we'll provide a general outline of various techniques. Remote viewing, researchers assert, can be done by anyone. No special talent is needed. Choose the techniques that work best for you.

The most important factor in remote viewing is a willingness to succeed at it. Accept the possibility.

To begin, you will need paper and pencils or pens. A tape recorder is optional. A comfortable seat, well lit, where you can write or draw is best.

Choose an assistant to select your targets. The assistant will determine the target location or, if you are using small objects, will place the objects at sites of the assistant's choice. Use someone you trust who is supportive.

Initially, have the assistant choose a simple target, telling you only that a target has been chosen—not what the target is. The target may be the letter *A* on a piece of paper, a screwdriver, or any recognizable small item.

Sit down. Quiet your mind. Envision yourself succeeding in this attempt. Allow your body and mind to totally relax. Don't try to attract the information, just allow it to enter your mind. Have your pencil ready.

As thoughts or images come to mind, sketch them quickly. Don't attempt to fill in details. Capture impressions. If you wish, write words or short sentences. Don't analyze the information you're receiving.

If you have a tape recorder, record stream-of-consciousness impressions. Say whatever comes into your mind. Be open to all sensations. Record whatever occurs. Include things you feel, hear, taste, smell, or think about.

Again, don't strain; don't analyze: allow the information to come to you. Stop when you're tired. No single session should exceed fifteen minutes.

Next, have your assistant reveal the true nature of the target. Go to the target site and observe the target yourself. Take your papers or recording along. As you confirm your impressions by feedback on-site, emphasize your hits—your correct perceptions. This builds confidence. If your descriptions are close to the actual target, try to remember how you felt when you were describing the target. Try to recapture those feelings during subsequent remote viewings.

Feedback is very important to this process. The Russian experimenter Nina Kulagina found that when she was denied feedback about an object she'd viewed, her results suffered.

Continue practicing in early sessions with nearby targets. Select experiments that can be done and verified quickly to facilitate feedback and reinforce positive results. Remember o remain positive and choose coworkers who are enthusiastic.

Once you are sure of your fundamental skills, you may wish to work with an outbound viewer, or on-site observer. This on-site observer will go to the target at the appropriate time and stay there, looking around, for a few minutes. This on-site observer should be supportive of the project, someone with an appropriate belief system and reality map for remote viewing.

The on-site observer should carefully note the surroundings of the target area. Jack Houck reports a case where a remote viewer described an area initially deemed a complete miss. Later evaluation of the target area revealed that the remote viewer correctly identified the area to the *rear* of the on-site observer, who was looking in the opposite direction!

Other experimenters have noted right and left reversals during early experiments, as well as size distortions. Make sure that the chosen area has unique, significant detail. Recognizable areas provide the remote viewer the best target.

You may choose to add a third person to your party at this point, who will ask you questions as you attempt remote viewing. To assist in this, we have appended (Appendix A) a list of thirty questions developed by Jahn and Dunne at Princeton University.

These thirty questions are designed to elicit responses from the remote viewer that help identify the target. Appendix B is a checklist used in remote viewing at Princeton.

To conduct a three-person experiment, have your on-site observer go to a site of his or her choosing at a predetermined time. You and the interviewer will remain at another site. Neither you nor the interviewer should know the target the observer has selected.

At the designated time, clear your mind. Describe your impressions to the interviewer. Sketch drawings. Respond to the interviewer's questions. When you have completed the experiment, go to the site with the interviewer and observe it. Ask the on-site observer to meet you and to stand in the exact position from which he or she observed the site. Note the surroundings for similarities to features you described.

You may conduct such an experiment any number of times, always selecting a new target, to build confidence in your skill. The results may surprise you.

Sometimes, experienced remote viewers can work without feedback and without on-site observers. Janet Morris has trained a few remote viewers for cold calls: independently gathered, quick responses without any subsequent feedback as to what the information she's asking for means or whether the viewers were correct. While doing site verification for Richard Groller in 1988, using a site plan drawn from an overflight photo and a blowup of a piece of equipment on the site, Morris made an error and gave one of her remote viewers two copies of the piece of equipment and no copy of the site plan.

The remote viewer gave Morris a detailed description of the site plan, which was highly unusual, specific in detail and nature, and which he did not have and could not have seen.

In 1980, Jack Houck was conducting a series of remote viewing experiments. Included in his target list were the coordinates 52 degrees, 43 minutes, 37 seconds north latitude; 174 degrees, 5 minutes, 49 seconds east longitude. It is fair to say that very few people in the Los Angeles area, where the exercise was conducted, could mentally transcribe those coordinates to a given location from memory.

Those coordinates equate to the position of Cobra Dane, an isolated site on Shemya, a tiny island far out in the Aleutian chain belonging to Alaska. Cobra Dane is a U.S. technical-intelligence collection facility with a large phased-array radar, designed to track Soviet reentry vehicles during ICBM tests. This facility, built by Raytheon Corporation, can also track satellites as they orbit the earth. Details about Cobra Dane were released by the U.S. government in 1976 to demonstrate that it was not an anti-ballistic-missile radar, which would have violated the ABM treaty then in effect.[14]

During the experiment, the remote viewer, blind to the target selected except for the coordinates provided to him, described the following:

"Either a mesa or a plateau."

"I could see an edge, so I knew there was a drop in the land."

"It's isolated. Desolate."

"I could smell sweet grass and there were small wildflowers."

"Felt cool, almost cold at times."

"Marker [sketch 2] doesn't seem natural because it's symmetrical: landing."

"Impression of a landing site."

"Sense the ocean . . . might be able to see it looking off this cliff."

"I see a man, a technician of some sort. Standing next to either a weather instrument or piece of a radar."

"Measuring light from the sun."

"Receivers, part of the chain is also senders."

"Waves of some sort. It's not radio waves. It's not signals in terms of messages, although I feel something is being sent out and received, and most of the metering of the equipment is not done there on the site."

"That piece of equipment is sort of on the edge of that plateau."

Example 3 consists of a drawing of the Cobra Dane site and four sketches drawn by the subject.

The remote viewer in this case was a nontechnical person. It is readily apparent that the amount of detail provided indicates this person was accurately describing the selected target site. Consider what data might have been gathered had the remote viewer been a trained technician who also had these skills. The intelligence-gathering components of many governments around the world find the possibility of remotely gathered information about their most sensitive facilities—and the facilities of rival governments—both alluring and distressing. For intelligence purposes, remote viewing promises a lower level of risk than either human or technical penetration. It is virtually undetectable. Remote-viewing invasions cannot be countered by conventional means. And the quality of the information gathered is no more suspect, in many cases, than what is gathered from human foreign sources.

Project Scanate and other experiments demonstrated that information can be received about a location by just identifying it, using a mechanism such as a universal transverse mercator (UTM) projection.[15] This also implies you can acquire information about a designated target area without physically going to that site.

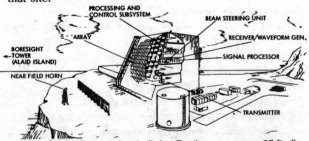

Giant Cobra Dane radar, built by Raytheon, uses a 95-ft.-dia. phased array with a sloping face angled 20 deg. above the horizontal to provide vertical coverage up to 80 deg. Radar, operating in L-band, is designed to detect reentry vehicles at distances of 2,000 naut. mi. and larger satillites at altitudes up to 25,000 naut. mi.

COBRA DANE REMOTE VIEWING EXPERIMENT

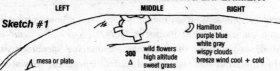

Sketch #1

"I could see an edge, so I knew there was a drop in the land. It's isolated. Desolate."

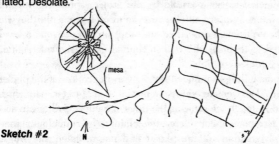

Sketch #2

"Marker doesn't seem natural because it's symmetrical. I see a man, a technician of some sort, standing next to either a weather instrument or a piece of radar."

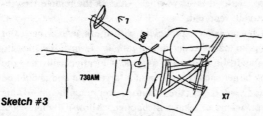

Sketch #3

"Receiver, part of the chain, is also sender . . . that piece of equipment is sort of on the edge of that plateau."

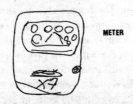

Sketch #4

"Waves of some sort. It's not radio waves. It's not signals in terms of messages, although I feel that something is being sent out and received and most of the metering of the equipment is not done there on the sight."

SKETCHES COURTESY OF JACK HOUK

Complications arose from remotely viewing a site at Semipal-atinsk, a nuclear facility in Soviet Central Asia. The remote viewers described equipment that resembled the "accelerators and electron injectors" used in directed-energy experiments, hidden in an underground site. The remotely sensed information was rejected as not possible by the project sponsors. Several years later, Western intelligence sources learned the Soviets *had* the equipment described and were working beyond a level credited to them by the U.S. technical establishment. Again, the psychics were right.[16]

A most telling example of remote viewing concerns the planet Jupiter. The remote viewer reported that Jupiter had rings around it, much the same as the rings of Saturn. Carl Sagan and other astronomers considered this claim to be ridiculous, since their observations of the planet had not revealed any rings, although Jupiter's moons were well known. Voyager I, nine years later, transmitted telemetry clearly showing that Jupiter, like Saturn, really does have rings—just as the remote viewers had objectively reported.[17]

As you become more proficient with these techniques, you may attempt to master precognitive remote viewing. The on-site observer should be told *when* to go to a location and view the target. The target should come from a target pool and should be selected and visited *after* the remote viewer actually records his or her impressions of what will happen. Allow sufficient time between the *subjective* input of the remote viewer and the sub-sequent observation by the on-site observer, to ensure there is no direct overlap. The remote viewing should occur *well before* the site is observed by the on-site observer. At least an hour should be sufficient to ensure that no overlap will occur, al-though days or weeks will work just as well.

When looking at targets, there sometimes appears to be an attraction of the viewer to emotional events at the site. Jack Houck released a case in which the target location happened to be the grid coordinates of a sunken ship. The viewers reported a ship but one where chaotic activity was occurring and lives were being lost. They had apparently targeted the physical location of the ship, but at a time in the past, i.e., the highly emotional event of the ship's sinking. This emotional attraction has been anecdotally reported by a number of researchers. While emotion is very hard to quantify, it does appear to be consistent with the concept of the interconnectedness of the universe.

Experienced remote viewers say it is a matter of personal choice whether or not to allow emotional interaction while viewing selected sites and past events. These experienced remote viewers have observed tragic events and yet reported them objectively. To be objective one must view the site in a detached state. New remote viewers should be aware that they may encounter emotional events, and be prepared to deal with them.

To facilitate successful remote viewing, several groups, such as the Moebius Group, have gone to a consensual decision-making process: Several viewers are given the same target, area, object, or event. Judges evaluate the work of all viewers. Then, by using a questionnaire similar to the one in Appendix A, they evaluate the information and derive statistical probabilities of accuracy. This consensual method greatly enhances the probability of success, compared to the performance of a given individual on a continuous basis. On rare occasions, an individual may be correct and the group incorrect. Still, experienced remote viewers confirm that the best way to improve the success ratio is to use consensus.

Sometimes, individuals who are frequently correct have periods when they miss the target completely. At times, subjects may be just as confident about the accuracy of information that turns out to be incorrect—or not verifiable—as they are about information that proves to be valid. The group-consensus method allows a researcher to obtain results that are less dependent on an individual's state of mind on any one occasion.

A recent addition to the field of remote sensing has been a process known as associative remote viewing, or ARV. This process received a lot of attention with some of the early experiments of Russell Targ and Keith Harary. They applied the ARV technique to predicting the outcome of the silver commodities market. As the commodity markets tend to fluctuate greatly from day to day, the application of the technique to this area would give them quick results and, if successful, would allow an investor to make substantial amounts of money. In fact, their very first attempt to do so was quite successful, as was reported in *The Wall Street Journal*.[18]

In the fall of 1982, their group (appropriately named Delphi Associates) decided to use ARV to forecast the fluctuations of the commodity known as December silver. Of nine forecasts made, seven were traded on the price of silver three days in the future. In each case, the magnitude and direction of the market were correctly predicted using this technique. The odds against this occurring by chance are 250,000 to 1.

To apply ARV, the viewer is required to look *forward* into time to determine what the outcome of an event will be. Rather than viewing the event itself, the viewer makes an association between a positive or negative outcome with specific items. For instance, if the stock market were to go up at a specific time, the outbound viewer would observe a predesignated target indicative of a positive result. Conversely, if the market went down, the viewer would see a second object with an associative value for a decrease in the market. The remote viewer, or viewers in this case, would be blind to all of the target pool. The process is normally done by having a group of viewers "go" forward to a specific point in time and try to determine what object will be observed—the target associated with a positive result or the target associated with a negative result. The viewers remain blind to the rest of the experiment and report their information back to investors. If the investors receive sufficient input of a target indicating a rise in the market, they then invest. If the object reported indicates a drop in the market, they can either sell or determine to ride it out. Of course investment is very risky, and in order to be successful you must hit well above the 50 percent level, since there are brokerage percentage fees involved.[19]

And Nothing Will Be Hidden from You: Remote Viewing

As of this writing, the responses to associative remote viewing when attached to finances have been mixed. It has been noted that when the fund-raising was motivated by altruism rather than greed, the results were seen positively. This has not yet been proven at a statistically significant level.

Jack Anderson reported in his column in *The Washington Post* that the military used remote viewing to successfully find a downed aircraft in Africa. Both U.S. and Soviet agents were frantically looking for the aircraft, and a U.S. remote viewer was able to provide enough accurate information to direct the American search team to within several kilometers of the crash site and beat the Soviet team to recovery.[20]

Many of the "star" remote viewers tend to undergo major changes in their life. Once they understand the interconnectedness of the universe, they sometimes lose interest in some of the more mundane aspects of remote viewing. As one experienced viewer put it: "Once you have seen how the universe really works, you lose interest in things like stealing secrets."

The Soviets may recently have encountered problems in obtaining individuals willing to participate in research designed to psychically influence others.[21] One unidentified psychic is quoted on film as telling Soviet psi researchers, "I will never do your dirty work." This type of response from gifted subjects may influence the future of Soviet research and development in the field of psychotronics.

This would be a welcome change from the pre-glasnost course of experimentation in the Soviet Union which, for years, has concentrated on the more sinister aspects of psi research. For example, Nikolai Kokolov, an ex-KGB agent, reported a case in which the spinal column of a human subject, in a laboratory in southern Russia, was fractured psychotronically from a distance. If this story is true, it represents a dramatic increase in psi capability, well above the demonstrated norm in the Western world.[22]

An extension of remote viewing, familiar to some readers, is known as out-of-body experience, or OOBE. Since Robert Monroe's landmark book *Journeys Out of the Body*[23] was published, many other books on the subject of out-of-body experiences have been written. Some believe it is possible that millions of people have had the experience of being disassociated from their bodies (often during a near death experience, or NDE) while retaining self-awareness. Monroe talks about going to a number of different dimensional localities while in this mental state. He reported traveling to distant sites and obtaining accurate information about ongoing activities at precise times.[24]

While OOBE has been widely reported, it remains highly controversial. Our intent at this point is not to further the controversy but to raise your awareness. It seemingly *does* happen to many people, and they firmly deny that it is any sort of mental aberration. In a number of cases, a person traveling out-of-body accurately retrieved information about another location, in the same detail as reported using other remote-viewing methodologies. In some cases, people have even reported being able to perturb a target area in such a way that others were aware of their out-of-body presence.[25]

A major experiment in this field was conducted by Alex Tanous and Karlis Osis at the American Society of Psychical Research in New York. During this experiment, Osis was required to move in an out-of-body state from one location, where his physical body was guarded, to another room and observe targets by standing at a specific location in the room. This target was *optically generated:* If viewed from a location other than the designated target site, it could not be seen. He reported correctly identifying 114 out of 177 targets during this series of experiments, clearly indicating that he was accurately retrieving data on a rather consistent basis.[26]

Some information gathered during remote viewing is clearly correct, while other information does not seem to apply to the designated target. Before acting on remote-viewing data, cross-correlate it with any other information at hand—eyewitness accounts, media reports, background information—to increase accuracy. Correlating your data with conventionally gathered information may allow you to make the requisite connections to solve the puzzle. If your remote-viewing data persistently seems to contradict all other reports and assumptions, do not discard it out of hand: It may in the end be proved right.

Often, firsthand reports are so colored by the assumptions and emotions of observers that the reports themselves may unintentionally prove misleading. Consider the following use of remote viewing to locate a lost object, one of its handiest everyday applications.

In the winter of 1989, Janet Morris met two couples for a dinner date. Shortly after entering the restaurant, one of the other women exclaimed that she'd lost her diamond bracelet "somewhere in the parking lot." She was certain she'd had it when she got out of the car.

Morris said, "It's down between the passenger seat of the car and the console, on the left." The woman denied that this could be possible. She and her husband argued. A search of the parking lot ensued. Morris once more said that she thought it was in the car, beside the seat. The next day, the bracelet was found there.

The experienced remote viewer can often perform such mundane location tasks on the spot, without prior preparation. One can, if one wishes, keep tabs on a spouse or child, track the progress of a package, or remotely view a baby in the womb and make a determination as to its sex.

When you are remote viewing in uncontrolled conditions and not as an experiment, it clouds the issue to discuss the mechanism at work. If you perceive the location of a lost object, say merely, "Have you thought of looking in such and such a place?" Keep score privately, if you wish. Sometimes you will be wrong, especially where emotionally charged events are involved. In such cases as straying spouses, try not to make matters worse.

Where your own emotions are involved, go carefully. Use

another viewer. Don't act on remotely viewed information with personal implications if that information can't be corroborated unless you're certain that your remotely viewed information is not distorted by your fears or doubts.

Use your head to keep your remote-viewing experiences from hurting others. If you're trying to find your friend's lost dog and you see it lying lifeless on the ground, we strongly suggest not telling your friend that the dog is dead.

The military applications of remote viewing were first discussed in a military journal by John Alexander in 1980. In that article, Alexander discussed both strategic and tactical uses.[27] If one can view any site, one can enter an adversary's headquarters and view operational plans. One can check the disposition and activity of troops against reports from conventional sources. Strategically, with the increasing need for treaty verification, remote viewing could assist in arms-control verification. As with all intelligence-gathering systems, such data must be correlated with all other known data, not used independently.

Applications of remote viewing to industrial espionage are not unthinkable. If remote viewing were used during early research and development phases, the target company would be without even the hypothetical protection of patent application.

These ethical difficulties are not unlike those involved with the introduction of any other new, invasive technology. Ethical issues of remote viewing will be settled on an ad-hoc basis by practitioners, whether or not a consensus of behavior eventually evolves.

The majority of researchers in this field come to the conclusion that there is an interconnectedness among all things. This premise has major implications for our beliefs and behaviors. Proponents of this concept suggest that information—in the form of consciousness—is a common ingredient throughout the universe. This universal interconnectedness may be the vehicle that allows remote viewing to operate.

And Nothing Will Be Hidden from You: Remote Viewing

In the arsenal of the warrior, who must remain alert to all threats and diligently gather as much information as possible, remote viewing is an incomparable weapon. It can alert you to threats at any distance, at any time, providing you with a qualitative edge over your enemies.

9

ACCESSING POWER: THE MIND/BODY INTERFACE

To maintain optimum performance, a warrior must be a totally integrated unit of mind, body, and spirit.

In the early 1900s, the Tibetan scholar Alexandra David-Neel studied the potentials of mind-body integration. Traveling about Tibet, David-Neel came across a centuries-old art called lung-gom. Lung-gom is actually a number of practices that combine mental concentration and breathing techniques to produce great physical stamina in such areas as long-distance running. She reported that a monk covered three hundred miles in thirty hours without stopping to eat or rest—an average of ten miles per hour over mountainous Tibetan terrain. This equates to maintaining a six-minute-mile pace for thirty consecutive hours.[1]

During her travels, David-Neel saw lung-gom practitioners running. On one occasion, she moved to a position where she could see into one of the runners' eyes. He appeared calm, his wide-open eyes fixed on some distant object. David-Neel reported that he seemed to lift himself off the ground with each leap, and rebound each time his feet hit the ground as if imbued with the elasticity of a ball. As the monk bounced, he appeared to be in a trance and did not even notice David-Neel as he passed by. When David-Neel asked about the training, the Tibetan monks reluctantly discussed special breathing techniques, learned over a three-and-a-half-year period and practiced in total darkness. When their training was complete, these monks could leap substantial distances in the air, beginning from a cross-legged, seated position.

David-Neel was told that the runners went into a trance before beginning to run, and if a runner broke trance suddenly, he might die. Training to develop superior physical and mental states made these extraordinary feats possible. Amazing things can happen when the efforts of body and mind are totally integrated.

A more contemporary advocate of mind/body integration is Tom Landry, formerly of the Dallas Cowboys. When asked about their training program, he emphasized two things: 1) Minimums are not enough—to be a champion takes more than maintaining a minimal or respectable standard. Both strength and endurance are needed to approach the maximum potential required to produce a winning team. 2) A high level of physical conditioning pays off in other areas. When in top form, the players maintain enhanced self-confidence, increased alertness, and more aggressive and competitive attitudes.[2]

Most of us do not train to be long-distance runners or professional football players. Nonetheless, exercise is vitally important to our body-mind balance. It is estimated that only one out of four city dwellers gets enough exercise. This may be a major contributing factor to increases in heart disease, obesity, and other health problems.[3]

The military has an obvious interest in physical fitness. All services employ basic training, during which new recruits are brought to an acceptable level of fitness. Many recruits are far below acceptable standards and must be brought up safely and quickly. After basic training, some join units requiring very high degrees of physical training, such as Army Rangers, Airborne, and Special Forces units, Navy SEALS, Marine Recon teams, and Air Force Combat Control teams. This is not a one-stop test. Today, most units require physical-fitness testing on a routine basis, for every level.

EXERCISE TYPES

The three major types of exercise are known as aerobic, isometric, and isotonic.[4] Aerobic exercises, such as running, jogging, swimming, or dancing, increase your oxygen intake. Aerobic exercise increases the heart and respiratory rates, delivering more oxygen to the body and increasing cardiovascular fitness. Effective results from aerobic activity require that you reach and maintain a desirably elevated heart rate for twenty minutes during each training session.

Isometric exercises increase strength by exerting muscles against an immovable force. To try isometrics, push against a wall or door jamb, or push or pull on one hand with the other, exerting equal and opposite force.

Isotonics increases strength and builds muscles by such methods as weight lifting. These exercises can be used either for building bulk and strength or for developing muscle tone. Isotonic exercise exerts muscles against a movable force.

There is some special equipment that integrates isometric with isotonic exercise. The advantage of an isometric workout is that you need no special equipment.

Before beginning any strenuous exercise program, consult a physician and physical conditioning experts to determine the type of exercise that best fills your needs. Before engaging in aerobic exercises, monitoring your heart rate will be important. A good rule of thumb is to subtract your age from 220 beats, and then take 80 percent of that remainder as your maximum heart rate. Some suggest a heart rate of only 70 percent is the highest rate that should be held for a period of at least twenty minutes to get the maximum benefit. If you show any unusual symptoms or have pain, stop immediately and consult a doctor.

For the vast majority of people, starting an exercise program is the hardest part. Begin by establishing the goals of your training: improved health; weight reduction; looking or feeling better; or participating in specified sports events. Set your goals in both long- and short-term categories so that you can pace attainment incrementally, at milestones. Remember to use the visualization techniques and muscle memory you learned in Chapter 7. See yourself accomplishing the tasks you have set for yourself in a competent and easy manner by a specific time and while maintaining perfect health.

Be sensible. Before engaging in these training activities, ensure you have the proper equipment or clothing for participation. Have good shoes if you will be running, jogging, or engaging in other activities where your feet hit the floor with substantial impact. Always allow time to warm up beforehand. By stretching your muscles prior to exercise, you will avoid injury caused by abrupt strain. Allow a cool-down period after exercise. If you have unusual pain or distressing sensations, *stop* what you are doing and consult a health-care professional immediately.

Remember that as you are training, you are asking your body to make certain changes. Be aware of what your body is telling you and allow *it* to teach *you*. This is a form of body feedback. The three types of exercise we have outlined should not cause you extensive pain. A wise saying advises us to "train, not strain." You are looking for a gradual increase in your capabilities, a real and sustainable improvement in muscle memory, strength, and tone, as well as improved coordination and mind-body integration.

CROSS CRAWLS

Mental preparation for physical activity can be as important as physical preparation. How many times, when you were determined to run a certain distance, has that distance seemed simply too far to go? What you have experienced is an illusion of difficulty. This is an inability to break the task into bite-size bits.[5]

A simple mental strategy can overcome this problem. Consider the story of the Russian weight lifter at the Olympics: The weight lifter was going after the world record. He *knew* he had not broken the record before, and his trainers were concerned about his mental state. The trainers told the weight lifter that the weight was actually slightly less than the real weight, well within a weight he'd lifted on a previous occasion. The weight lifter, believing the weight was lighter than it really was, went out and lifted the weight, setting a world's record. The difficulty was only an illusion, established by his personal belief system.

In addition to visualization techniques, reality mapping, your targeting list, and your success space in which you can create images of the desired goal, you can also use special physical exercises to enhance mind-body integration. These exercises are based on our scientific understanding of brain function. We know there is cross-lateralization, i.e., the right hemisphere of the brain controls the left side of the body and the left hemisphere of the brain controls the right side of the body. We also know there is hemispheric specialization of the brain: certain areas of the brain appear to control specific functions.

These exercises are called cross crawls.[6] A simple cross crawl is a movement in which the arms swing freely and the right arm is raised at the same time the left leg is moved forward. The second half of the movement is to move the left arm and the right leg simultaneously. The simplest form of this exercise begins with the individual standing straight, head up, resting squarely on the shoulders, and then repeatedly doing the cross-crawl movements. The upper part of the body should be relaxed and free from tension and the knee should rise straight up and not cross the midline of the body. Actions should be free-flowing, relaxed, and free of stress. A classic example of cross crawl is walking or marching in place while allowing the arms to swing freely.[7]

As you can see, this is called a cross crawl because both sides of the body are operating simultaneously, thereby activating both the right and the left hemisphere of the brain. The counter to this is called homolateral movement. In that movement, the right arm and the right leg move at the same time, followed by the left arm and the left leg moving simultaneously. In homolateral crawling, only one side of the brain is being activated during movement.

Military marching is a form of cross-crawl exercise. Once learned, it helps units perform other tasks more efficiently. Cross crawls are beneficial for both physical performance, such as hand-eye integration, and for mental skills, such as reading.

The need for cross crawling comes from the specialization of the brain. In order to keep both sides, or both hemispheres, of the brain functioning simultaneously, you need to train the brain by doing such exercises as the cross crawl. This is one reason why having children go through a crawling phase is important. Many parents tend to push their children quickly to the walking phase and skip the phase of learning to crawl. Crawling is important not only for mobility but also for creating the channels to the corpus callosum that transfer the information from one hemisphere to the other, telling the brain to operate as an integrated unit.

Because cross crawls can improve one's physical skills, members of the military became interested in doing cross-crawl exercises. Traditional military exercises such as push-ups and pull-ups concentrate on one set of muscle groups but do very little to integrate movement. The one exception might be military running, but even at that, movement is relatively restricted as emphasis is placed on maintaining a group formation during execution. The discovery of integrated exercises, and their utility in Olympic training, led to the application of cross crawls in selected military elements, such as quick-response units and Special Forces, where physical dexterity is at a premium.

To maintain optimum physical condition, it is desirable to train, using both homolateral and crosslateral exercise.[8] A fully integrated person will be able to switch from one set to the other without difficulty. A good way to test this is to have an individual march in place starting out with cross-crawl or crosslateral exercises, i.e., the right arm and left leg coming up simultaneously, and vice versa. See how quickly the individual can change from one domain to the other. It may be best to have another individual work with you. Have the individual watch your activity and then suddenly give you the command to change. Responding to a second individual's commands will prevent you from thinking ahead; you have to see how quickly your mind can switch and accommodate the new activity. Seeing how fast you can make the change without stopping your legs will give you an indication of the cross-crawl and homolateral integration of your brain.

ADVANCED BREATHING TECHNIQUES

Like the food we eat or the water we drink, the air we breathe is critical to our survival. Just how we accomplish the act of breathing, however, can be of vital importance. To most Americans, breathing is something that is just done—you inhale and exhale. We may notice that we breathe sometimes faster and sometimes slower, but we generally pay very little attention to breathing.

Yet throughout history, the wisest of us have known that breath and specific breathing techniques are extremely important. They serve to integrate the mind, body, and spirit.

Studies using an electroencephalograph have recorded measurable effects during breathing exercises when subjects alternated nostrils for inhalation and exhalation. These studies demonstrate that specific areas of the mind can be activated by concentrated breathing through either nostril.[9]

Kundalini yoga had its origins in ancient India thousands of years ago. Over centuries of experimentation, yogis developed a profound understanding of the human nervous system and its functioning. Through the application of these techniques, they were able to govern self-regulation of the body and generate state-specific results. Through specific kinds of training, they were able to elicit and maintain states of their own choosing. Centuries later, studies in neuroscience are finally beginning to reveal the underlying mechanisms and substantiate the discoveries made so long ago. One important finding was the determination of the neuromatrix coupling mind and metabolism.[10]

The military application of kundalini yoga dates back over five thousand years, to the time when powerful individuals known as rishis developed (over generations) control and mastery of kundalini yoga. These practices were passed on through the Sikh warrior tradition for centuries. Famed were the soldiers of Guru Gobinde Singh, a great yoga of the late seventeenth and early eighteenth centuries in Punjab, India, whom he trained to be fearless in battle using kundalini yoga. Through these techniques, his soldiers were able to maintain a fearless attitude and display extraordinary proficiency on the battlefield. Their ability to go fearlessly into combat generated terror in the minds of their enemies.

Over time kundalini yoga, like many other disciplines, became highly specialized and divided. In this process, many techniques were lost as individual schools became wedded to the particular arts they applied. Only recently have certain teachers tried to recombine the scattered techniques, many of which remain closely guarded, proprietary secrets even today.[11]

In both military and civilian life, there are many potential applications of advanced breathing techniques. Fatigue is a factor common to all; this can be induced by excessive physical or mental stress and exacerbated by poor diet. Just as proper diet can help overcome fatigue, so too can the application of proper breathing techniques revitalize the body quickly.

Pilots of fighter aircraft must maintain sufficient cerebral blood flow during high G turns. The technique learned by American fighter pilots is to contract their abdominal muscles and hold their breath while in the turn. The application of kundalini-yoga skills offers improved performance in this area.[12]

Some of the more advanced techniques offer assistance in overcoming such problems as space-adaptation syndrome, changes in epidemiology through enhanced immunological competence of the body, as well as help in overcoming drug, alcohol, and other substance abuse.

In Chapter 2, "Quieting the Mind," we offered certain basic breathing techniques. We now offer some advanced techniques for expanding and balancing the mind.

EXERCISE 1: STRESS RELIEVER

The breathing pattern of this exercise provides immediate relief from stress by releasing tension accumulated throughout the day. For some people, this technique restores equilibrium to the central nervous system, heightens mental clarity, stimulates the metabolism, and provides renewed energy.

To begin, sit with the spine straight. Close your eyes and focus at the point where the nose meets the eyebrows. Inhale only through the nose, dividing the breath into eight equal parts. Inhale and exhale via full sets of eight parts at a rate of one to two parts per second. Continue to breathe in this pattern. Begin with a few minutes; five to ten is maximum at the beginning, and increase slowly over time until the maximum time of thirty minutes is reached. Completely relax, once you are finished.

Having completed the exercise, take inventory of how you feel. Be aware of your body, your mind, and the level of energy available to you.

Breathing is a bodily function most Americans take for granted. It is not a subject on which we place any degree of concentration, except when running, swimming, or engaging in other athletic activity. For the most part, we Americans fail to utilize the capacity of our lungs. We tend to inhale and exhale very shallowly. The ancient breathing techniques teach us to breathe deeply and exhale deeply, in order to remove all the stale or inactive air in the lungs and allow new, fresh, oxygenated air to enter the lungs. Practicing deep breathing *alone* can make a big difference in your quality of life.

EXERCISE 2: ALTERNATE BREATHING

You will remember in Chapter 2, we recommended you either inhale and exhale directly at a ratio of one to four or inhale, hold the air, and exhale at a ratio of one to four to two, building efficiency over time. We now address some other activities to enhance your breathing capacities.

One of the first advanced exercises is called alternate breathing. The body does this unconsciously, most of the time. Most people are not aware that they breathe predominantly through one nostril at a time. You can determine your primary nostril by holding a finger below your nose to feel which nostril expels the air. You actually rotate back and forth during the period of a day. Some yogis suggest that if you breathe continually through one nostril for more than twenty-four hours without changing, it may be a warning of impending illness.[13]

In this breathing exercise, you will use a single nostril. Begin with a cleansing breath. Sit with your spine straight, and close one nostril with your thumb. Inhale slowly and exhale slowly through the same nostril. The proportion should be one count inhale for every two counts exhaling. Do this initially for five to ten minutes.

Once you have practiced single-nostril breathing sufficiently to be comfortable with it, move on to the next step: alternating breaths. To do this, close one nostril with your thumb, breathe in; then close that nostril, release the other, and exhale. Immediately upon exhaling, breathe in through that same nostril; then close it and exhale through the first nostril. Again, the proportion of inhale to exhale should be one count inhaling for every two counts exhaling.[14]

To do full alternate breathing, you must add a retention step. To do this, inhale through one nostril; hold; and then exhale through the other nostril, again using your thumb and other finger to alternately close the nostrils. A full cycle would be to inhale through the right nostril; hold for a count of four times the inhalation; then release and exhale through the same nostril. Immediately upon exhaling, inhale through the left nostril; hold again for four times the inhalation; then exhale through the first nostril at two times the inhalation. Again the ratio would be one to four to two. At first, inhale for four seconds; hold sixteen seconds; and exhale eight seconds. Should you find the retention to be too long, you may modify it to a one-to-two ratio. Gradually increase the ratio until you inhale eight seconds; hold thirty-two seconds; exhale 16 seconds.[15]

A number of other more advanced breathing techniques can be learned after one has mastered the alternate-breathing practice. Should you decide to go forward, it is best to do so under the guidance of an experienced instructor.

JET LAG

Many of us have trouble maintaining our systems adequately in a static environment. Today's schedules have the business traveler flying great distances, often transcontinentally. One result may be a relatively modern phenomenon known as jet lag. Centuries ago, when people traveled by boat or by horse, there was no need to worry about biological changes taking place during movement, no matter what the distance. Nowadays, it is common to suffer from so-called jet lag, which is a desynchronization of the body's internal biological rhythms.

This is of great concern to the military, where large numbers of troops must move great distances and arrive in a combat-ready condition. Although business travelers may not be expected to arrive fit to fight, they are frequently expected to arrive in Europe or in Asia relatively rested and prepared to work on the local schedule.

Many travelers notice how these changes in their biological clock impair their ability to work. Flying from east to west appears to be easier than flying from west to east. This has to do with the greater desynchronization that occurs in west-to-east flight, of the light-and-dark cycle from your present time zone.

The desynchronization of your internal rhythmic functions (also called circadian rhythms) impacts your cognitive, intellectual, and physical processes. You will be likely to function at only 80 to 85 percent of your capacity. Normally, it takes two to three days for you to readjust in a new time zone. Unfortunately, today's business traveler frequently flies from the United States to Europe for two or three days and then returns. Frequent flyers generally notice the resulting misalignment.

In response to this problem, researchers at Walter Reed Army Medical Center, at the Walter Reed Army Institute for Research, elected a number of studies and have come up with suggestions for beating or minimizing the impact of jet lag. They suggest you begin preparing a day before your trip. Shift your sleep period: if you are westbound, go to bed one to two hours later than usual; if you are eastbound, go to bed one or two hours earlier. Eat three regular meals with no snacks, minimize caffeine intake, and avoid alcohol.[16]

On your departure day, eat very little during the day. Walter Reed recommends eating fruit as opposed to other sugary items. During the flight, drink two to three glasses of fluids every four hours (again avoiding alcohol). Sleep is recommended starting at around 10:00 P.M., and attempting to wake, around 6:00 A.M. Sleep on aircraft is recognized to be difficult, but it is not impossible. We will recommend another approach to that problem shortly. Once you are in flight, start to do things on your *destination*'s time.

Once at your destination, do everything possible according to the local time. A high-protein lunch is recommended and a large, high-carbohydrate dinner. This will help you sleep at night. Maximize your social and outdoor schedule to keep active. If you can, avoid taking a nap once you get there; this assists your resynchronization and alignment to the sleep pattern of the area.

The Walter Reed study suggests that during flight, you may take 100 milligrams of Dramamine about thirty minutes prior to your designated sleep period. Dramamine is an over-the-counter drug frequently used to control motion sickness. As a side effect, it causes drowsiness.

An alternative to drug-induced sleep has been developed by

Monroe Institute. Mentioned earlier, Robert Monroe was instrumental in developing a hemisync process that some people use to help induce out-of-body or altered consciousness states. The hemisync process, as Monroe calls it, for hemispheric synchronization of the brain, is based on auditory input going into your ears through a headset. Again, this is a matter of two different sounds at slightly different frequencies being heard causing an introduced frequency following response (FFR) in the human brain. [17]

Monroe has designed two tapes that help the brain establish the normal sleep pattern. The first tape is called the *Catnapper*.

During normal sleep, brain-wave frequencies cycle through bands measured in Hertz (Hz). Hertz means cycles per second. The wide-awake state, called beta, extends from fourteen to twenty-one cycles and may go higher during extreme stress. The alpha, or light-sleep state, usually associated with rapid eye movement (REM), extends from seven to thirteen cycles. The deep-sleep, or theta state, extends from three to seven cycles per second. Below three cycles is the delta state, which is the unconscious state. A normal sleep cycle starts from beta, goes down through alpha, and sometimes even into delta. It then goes back up again to the alpha or the low beta range. This forty-five-minute cycle occurs periodically; throughout the night, you are operating in these various modes. During a night of normal sleep, you will have four or five of these cycles and then awaken after gradually coming up through alpha to the beta state.

All phases of the cycle are necessary for a complete rest. Monroe has successfully compressed the full forty-five minute cycle into a twenty-five-minute guidance tape that tricks the brain into believing it has had a complete rest cycle. This tape can be used on short airline flights or whenever you require a refreshing nap in a relatively short time frame.

The second tape, *Deep Sleeper*, merely establishes a normal sleep cycle. Instead of waking you at the end (as does *Catnapper*), it allows you to drift off into a normal sleep cycle and awake on your own. This is useful for people who have trouble falling asleep but don't want to use drugs. The tapes are available through the Monroe Institute.[18]

QUICK FIXES

Today's warrior and business manager both spend a great deal of time reading. When reading lengthy documents, many invariably fall asleep. Some people even use reading as a technique to induce sleep. To acquire and retain data from reading, you must be awake and alert.

The way our eyes move back and forth during reading can fatigue eye muscles, causing drowsiness. To counteract this, place one hand on your navel with the fingers of the other hand just below the clavicle, to either side of your chest's midline. You'll be amazed to see how quickly alertness returns and you can continue reading.[19]

Here is a quick-reaction technique for the individual who is under emotional pressure but still must concentrate on matters at hand: Simply place one or two fingers about one inch above your eyebrow near the outside of your forehead. Mentally review the distressful circumstance. Repeat this process two or three times. The impact of the stressor will lessen dramatically, allowing you to refocus on business.[20]

In the military, it is said that amateurs talk of battles and tactics while professionals talk of logistics. It is time to hone your warrior's edge.

10

BIOFEEDBACK: TUNING CONSCIOUSNESS

Biofeedback techniques may help the warrior acquire and maintain maximum human performance. A relatively modern science, it was officially born in 1962, but it's really been around much longer. Biofeedback is what we call any mechanism that externally verifies controlled, physical changes occurring within the body. Several different instruments and techniques exist that monitor biological processes. Through feedback, we can learn to control our bodies in new ways.

Some of the instruments for monitoring the body in biofeedback include the electromylograph (EMG), which monitors muscle tension; thermometers, which monitor skin temperature; galvanic skin response (GSR) meters, which monitor the electrical resistance of the skin. Other systems monitor brain waves; these have led to some of the more sophisticated and controversial work in the field.

Testing has conclusively demonstrated that biofeedback training can assist in skill acquisition. In a clinical setting, biofeedback has helped people overcome stress, anxiety, phobia, traumatic events, learning disabilities, behavioral disorders, psychological disturbances, medical ailments, and even substance abuse.

The principle of biofeedback is very simple, but its technological instrumentation can be very complex. In principle, biofeedback instruments reflect—or feed back to the individual—information about activity occurring inside the mind or body.

Seemingly involuntary physical states, such as muscle tension in the neck, can be electronically monitored as nearly simultaneous visual or auditory signals. Employing biofeedback, one may learn to modify behavior or physical states by controlling the intensity of the monitored sound or sight.

For instance, in monitoring muscle tension using an EMG device, feedback indicating the muscle's state is presented as an auditory signal. Relaxing that muscle diminishes the sound. You learn to diminish the sound by relaxing the muscle, thus acquiring control over the internal mechanisms that can relax the muscle. Using sound indicators, you may then identify and catalog the internal control mechanism that relaxes the muscle and releases the tension. Once the conscious mind can monitor, evaluate, and modify a physical state, connections between the biofeedback signal and one's thoughts and feelings become apparent. These connections teach us how we react to challenges and stress. As we understand these connections, we learn how to control our reactions to everyday stressors. With increased self-control comes a broader reality map and freedom to access our true potential as enhanced human beings.

Athletes have improved their performance using biofeedback. In 1980, D. J. DeWitt reported on two studies—one on a group of football players, the other on a group of basketball players. Reviewing the use of biofeedback to lower the very high stress levels experienced in basketball players before or after games, he found significantly lowered heart rates for participating players. The coaches of the respective teams felt that players' individual performances were enhanced during the game whenever biofeedback had been used beforehand. Players reported feeling generally more relaxed and in greater control during the game. Colloquially, they felt "looser" during competition. Injury rate was lower for players who had undergone the biofeedback training.[1]

A biathlon requires the participant to ski cross-country as rapidly as possible and then quickly come to a stop and fire a rifle. The major problem for championship-level shooters is learning to shoot literally between heartbeats to maintain the steadiest position possible. Biofeedback was used to teach the individuals exactly when to squeeze the trigger; how to slow down the heart rate after the high stress skiing. Performance scores have improved significantly in recent years, since a number of countries have employed biofeedback training, as well as visualization, to increase their teams' biathlon capabilities.[2]

Biofeedback has been used for muscle training in the world of music. Stringed-instrument players improved performance by learning to recognize and produce the optimum level of tension in specific muscles.

Although most of the heart-rate-related biofeedback research has concentrated on medical therapy applications, the National Research Council (NRC) report entitled *Enhancing Human Performance* suggests that healthy human subjects can enhance their physical capacity, realizing a greater economy of energy during hard physical work. This would have direct relevance for the military or for anyone concerned with optimizing effort while performing physical labor.[3]

Additional military applications include using biofeedback to control blood circulation in troops exposed to extremes of climate for long periods of time, as well as controlling more general physical parameters when under severe stress. Some fighter pilots and astronauts already have used biofeedback training to help control pulse and heart rate.

Like heart rate, respiration can be monitored and the results fed back to the individual. Respiration biofeedback may alter and improve the metabolic efficiency of intensely trained athletes.

Biofeedback: Tuning Consciousness

A popular use for biofeedback is in the regulation of body temperature. Medical professionals have used thermal training to treat vasoconstrictive disorders such as migraine headaches, frostbite, or Reynaud's disease. Patients learn to mentally control the temperature in various parts of their body. Relatively untrained individuals were able to warm their hands several degrees merely by thinking about warm hands.[4]

In the early 1970s, at a conference in Hawaii, John Alexander learned a field expedient method of thermal self-regulation from Dr. Barbara Brown, a prominent biofeedback researcher. To demonstrate biofeedback-enhanced control of bodily functions, Dr. Brown used a number of very small thermometers gauged to measure human body temperature. After taping these thermometers to their fingertips and recording a baseline temperature, individual participants tried to affect the temperature readings. Shortly, each participant had learned to exert a significant amount of thermal control.

Such techniques have obvious benefits for those who work in cold climates. Once trained to increase the heat of their hands, they can increase their physical dexterity and manipulative skills in cold weather—particularly helpful when performing tasks without gloves and where the skin is exposed to extreme temperature for short periods of time.[5]

A widely known medical application of biofeedback is in controlling migraine headaches. A migraine sufferer may be asked to concentrate on warming hands or other extremities in order to take blood flow away from the brain. This reduces the excessive blood flow to the brain that induces migraine headaches. Some researchers have found that conscious heating of extremities is a good way to relieve general tension.

Advanced biofeedback training should be undertaken under the direct supervision of a trained professional. There is a wide range of instrumentation available to the general public. Some are very sophisticated and accurate systems; some are mass-produced at lower prices, offering limited accuracy. These devices should not be used for the treatment of medical ailments.

We recommend familiarizing yourself with professional biofeed-back trainers before purchasing an inexpensive device. Medical applications should be undertaken only under the control of a medical doctor or therapist.

Temperature training may be an area you choose to try on your own. Make sure the thermometer registers close to the body temperature. Apply the thermometer against the skin, maintaining close body contact with tape or an elastic band. First establish your baseline—i.e., see what your normal body temperature is. Then try to increase and decrease the temperature reading on the thermometer.

To do this, think of your hand becoming very warm. Imagine your hand being placed in warm water, under a blanket, or close to a fire. Visualize any situation that causes a feeling of heat in your arm or hand. Once successful, try cooling the hand. Think of putting your hand into cold water, on a block of ice, or in a refrigerator. Make it cold, and watch the temperature decline. Remember, you are learning to control the *change* in temperature. Note the internal feeling associated with success. Be aware of all physical sensations, not only around the thermometer, but throughout the rest of your body. Look for repeatable mental or emotional cues. Your goal is to consciously control body changes normally considered to be automatic.

Keep in mind that this thermometer method is not scientifically precise. It will give you a feel for the biofeedback response. This technique should not be used by a layman for medical problems. For the treatment of migraine headaches or other vascular constrictive diseases, consult a physician, who may choose to either provide biofeedback training or refer you to a trained therapist.

GALVANIC SKIN RESPONSE

Another form of traditional biofeedback training is known as galvanic skin response (GSR) or electrodermal response (EDR). The physiology being monitored here is the amount of moisture on the skin. Resistance goes down as moisture on the skin increases, indicating certain physiological states frequently associated with distress. GSR is one of the major readings used in the polygraph, or lie detector. In the classic polygraph operation, respiration, blood pressure, and GSR are monitored. Frequently, the GSR response will give the greatest indication of change in physiological distress. You may have encountered a version of GSR: sweaty palms when someone is lying.

Physical stress is often accompanied by an increased GSR response. In one stress-training method, an individual puts a band on one or two fingers. The band, attached to a monitoring device, feeds back physiological stress readings using audio frequencies. Many such devices are available, from fairly simple to very sophisticated GSR systems.

Dr. Jan Northup conducts strategic planning sessions for selected corporate managers. As part of the stress training in the program, trainees are introduced to the GSR device and allowed to use it during break periods. At one retreat, where Dr. Northup taught a laboratory director how to use the GSR device, the lab director tried bringing to mind his superiors while monitoring his GSR response. Certain names evoked a dramatic GSR response from his body.

On another occasion, three of the top people failed to return from the group's lunch break. Since this session could not continue without their critical participation, she finally went looking for them, and finally found the three of them sitting off by themselves, all attached to the small GSR devices. They were repeating to each other the names of various individuals, both inside and outside their organization, and listening to the tonal changes from the devices, thus allowing the GSR device to indicate exactly who induced significant stress in the organization. It was certainly an innovative application of GSR training.

These devices should not be used for the treatment of medical ailments. Those applications should be referred to a medical doctor or trained therapist.

AUTOGENIC TRAINING

Studies have indicated that biofeedback works best in combination with other techniques. One major training technique employed with biofeedback is known as autogenic training. This is a psychophysiological optimization and relaxation technique, originally developed in the 1930s by Dr. Johann Schultz and Wolfgang Luthe. The technique consisted of six standard exercises aimed at teaching an individual to create at will the sensations of heaviness; warmth; actual reduction of heart rate; change in respiration; apparent warming of the solar plexus; and cooling of the forehead. The modern version of this training program is called autogenic biofeedback training, or AFT.[6] This program, using techniques similar to those discussed in our discussion of visualization, consists of an instructor teaching the trainees to control the six factors by talking them through the process and helping them create a mental scene to stimulate the physiological responses.

AFT training has been investigated by NASA in solving the problem of space sickness. Studies indicate that AFT training could help people control the effects of motion sickness. For those who suffer from motion sickness, in aircraft or ships or automobiles, biofeedback and AFT may offer relief under the direction of a doctor or therapist.[7]

The U.S. is not the only country looking into the application of biofeedback training for space flight. In 1983, at a conference in Cambridge, England, then-Lieutenant Colonel John Alexander was one of the Americans who met with members of a delegation from the People's Republic of China. Representatives from the Chinese equivalent of NASA declared their interest in extended human performance research in preparation for manned space flight, and Alexander came away with the impression that they took these training programs very seriously. The Chinese delegation indicated their feeling that for extended space flight, a better understanding of and training for enhanced human performance would be required.

THE EEG CONTROVERSY

The most controversial aspect of biofeedback research has historically been the electroencephalograph, or EEG. Nevertheless, there has been a resurgence of this type of research during the last few years.[8]

In EEG biofeedback, researchers address the self-regulation of electrocortical responses of the brain. These are measured by devices ranging in degrees of sophistication and complexity, which record brain-wave activity normally broken into the four frequency bands we discussed in Chapter 9: 1) beta, the highest level of activity, with signals measuring above 14 Hz; 2) alpha, which usually ranges between 7 and 13 Hz; 3) theta, in the 3–7 Hz range and 4) delta, below 3 Hz.

EEG training and measurement is a very complex skill. Even arriving at a definition of the nature of the alpha state, where many believe creative activity takes place, is not as simple as many believe. Brain activity is terribly complex and the measurements are averaged over some distance, depending upon the placement of the electrodes on the brain.

Popular belief suggests that in untrained persons, physical and mental stress reduces the amount of alpha activity created by the brain. A number of experiments have corroborated a depression of alpha activity during periods of extreme stress. Many researchers who attempted to teach alpha-wave control discontinued their work after trainees failed to gain and maintain the desired levels of control.

At the Langley Porter Psychiatric Institute at the University of California-San Francisco Medical Center, successful brain-wave research was done under the direction of Dr. James Hardt. Dr. Hardt, through extensive experiments, discovered a mapping sequence for specific areas of the brain that related to specific psychological problems. He also found that increasing brain-wave activities was an effective way of combating stress and anxiety. Brain-wave activities relate *directly* to consciousness and to mental conditions.[9]

Finding the success or failure of alpha training dependent on two key variables—the design of electronic instruments for providing accurate alpha feedback; and optimized training protocols—Hardt established the Biocybernaut Institute, incorporating advanced biomedical research with microcomputerized electronic instruments to solve real problems for real people. He also developed protocols for training alpha-level brain-wave generation.

In September of 1983, then-Lieutenant Colonel Alexander and Lieutenant Colonel James MacLachlan were offered the opportunity to undergo some very specialized EEG training at Dr. Hardt's institute, under the auspices of the University of California-San Francisco Medical School. These techniques were designed initially to increase alpha activity in patients with problems, but Dr. Hardt has adapted them to increase the capabilities of normal, healthy individuals.

Hardt deduced a direct correlation between blood flow to the brain and alpha-wave activity, suggesting that blood flow to the brain impacts the ability to create alpha waves. Where blood flow is decreased or restricted, a commensurate decrease is seen in mental capabilities. Since the brain is the master regulator for the entire body, any deficiency in the delivery of oxygen and glucose to the brain—from illness or aging—will have far-reaching and cascading adverse effects. If hormonal, metabolic, and biochemical regulation systems are disrupted, the result may be digestive upset, reduction in intellectual functioning, even clinical anxiety and depression.

Some adverse effects seem to be reversible through the use of drugs and EEG biofeedback training. Studies indicate, in cases where the brain has not actually been damaged due to the lack of blood flow, normal psychic drive and intellectual capability appear to return to normal after therapy.[10]

In healthy people, the result of EEG training is enhanced creativity and mental control over physiology. In group situations, EEG trainees can create a state of coordination in which participants actually "think alike," as described in the experiment below.

BIOCYBERNAUT TRAINING

The training Alexander and MacLachlan underwent at the Biocybernaut Institute was divided into two phases.

During the first week, each subject was placed in a separate anechoic chamber. The chamber was dark and sound free. Each subject was instructed to generate alpha, and a score was posted at the end of each training episode. Throughout the session, each received audio feedback indicating whether alpha generation was increasing or decreasing.

In figure 3, the top chart's readings indicate brain-wave activity monitored on the first day. There is some alpha activity, but of relatively low amplitude and duration. Compare this with the bottom readings, taken on the seventh day. You will notice, even with an untrained eye, a significant difference in both the amount and amplitude of alpha activity generated by both Alexander and MacLachlan. Available statistical studies clearly show that the ability to control activity is trainable, and demonstrate that it can be increased on demand.

To initially increase alpha, both trainees were asked to tune their physiology to the center of the arousal spectrum—those stimuli that elicit a physiological response—to maximize their background alpha. The key to success in learning alpha increase was the ability to maintain a high level of resting arousal—remaining alert to select external stimuli while maintaining what is commonly known as a meditative state.

Beyond tuning the physiological arousal levels, alpha increase by the trainees seemed to depend upon their ability to increase blood flow to the brain. This is especially likely, since we seem to have a positive linkage between brain blood flow and the alpha activity of humans. The charts clearly indicate that both Alexander and MacLachlan were able to learn to control

Figure #3

Advanced EEG Feedback

Top chart, taken on first day of training

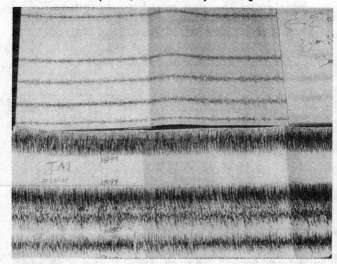

Bottom chart, showing increased alpha activity one week later.
PHOTO BY JOHN ALEXANDER

alpha enhancement with only a few days' training and could greatly increase their alpha output.

Through such training, older persons who have acquired superior experiences over an accumulated period of time could be trained to retain or regain their youthful creativity and intellectual capacity. Trained individuals could also adapt more readily to high-stress situations such as those encountered by the military and in the competitive industrial environment.

Trained individuals could more easily work in anxiety-producing environments of every sort, especially group environments, where anxiety communicates itself.

Because such training allows greater personal control of anxiety, it would be invaluable in the United States where, in 1973, Raskin and others estimated that 5 percent of the population of the United States was afflicted by chronic anxiety.[11]

Many of these chronically anxious people are high achievers, commanding positions of responsibility and authority, often unwilling to admit problems and unlikely to participate in any form of conventional therapy. This is especially true in the military, in cases of those with high-level security clearances. One of the standard questions in the government's background investigation asks whether or not the individual has ever sought assistance for any mental impairment.

The unique advantage of alpha brain-wave training is that it makes no judgments about the subject's mental or physical health. It is merely a method to enhance performance. In the training process, individuals may painlessly unlearn maladaptive responses to stress without having been treated "for any mental impairment."

All people can benefit from learning to increase their alpha output. A person does not have to be mentally ill to have small adverse elements in his or her personality. Hardt suggests the EEG training can help people normalize small personality dysfunctions and achieve healthier, more effective interpersonal relationships. A healthy person can drift into dysfunctionality by being continually exposed to stressful situations—and through normal aging. Older people are more prone to psychological dysfunction than younger people, and less adaptive to stressful situations. Alpha enhancement can improve adaptivity.

Hardt maintains that the combination of learning alpha enhancement, increasing and maintaining blood flow, and developing a low-anxiety state of "open" mindedness could be an important key to maintaining peak levels of youthful creativity far beyond even normal retirement age. This training could, he says, unleash a creative flood of brilliant innovations from corporate management, senior scientists, and political and military leaders.

During the second phase of their training, Alexander and MacLachlan were trained together. They entered the same anechoic chamber simultaneously. The EEG was wired separately from each individual but recorded on the same chart. Notice in figure 4 how the brain waves are not merely similar but almost identical. Alexander's brain waves seem to increase in amplitude, and slightly in speed, and directly to replicate those of MacLachlan. Clearly MacLachlan was driving the brain-wave patterning, for it is similar to the pattern he developed in the prior week.

This experiment suggests the potential for "entraining" the brain waves of two or more individuals. The potential for getting groups of individuals on task and working better together is extensive and exciting. Colloquially, our language has incorporated this idea for a long time. We talk about "getting on the same wave length," "getting our heads together," "tuning in," etc. The graphs above indicate that this precise effect may be controllable.

A personal dimension developed during these sessions. Both trainees noted that from time to time, secrets would "slip" from one person to another. Although this phenomenon was not specifically tested for, other people training together also found they sometimes would simultaneously—and nonverbally—acquire information about each other. We can infer from this both the potential of telepathic communication when brain

Figure #4

Advanced EEG Biofeedback—Brain-wave Entertainment

Top two lines: Alexander

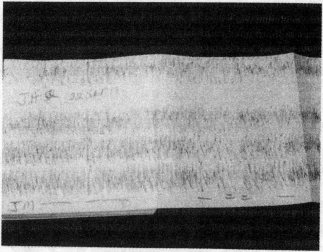

Bottom lines: Maclachlin

Although separately monitored by the EEG, note that the brain-wave patterns are almost identical. Key events are clearly indicated on all channels. PHOTO BY JOHN ALEXANDER

waves sync, and also that there must be trust and intimacy between individuals participating in this kind of training.

Hardt stated that MacLachlan and Alexander produced remarkable high-amplitude, nonartificial, simultaneous EEG events during their shared feedback training. Greater depths of intimacy may occur during brain-wave entrainment. The unexpected entrainment demonstrated by the subjects suggests that the brain-wave oscillations of electronic potentials may act as a harmonic oscillator. Hardt feels this shared feedback can both produce strong bonds between trainees and facilitate group coordination during assigned tasks.

Six months after the training ended, Hardt wrote a letter to Alexander saying a subcomponent experiment had been embedded in their training: In advance, Hardt had chosen one unwitting subject, in this case Alexander, for an experiment in telepathic suggestion. On the seventh day of the individual training (the last day the subjects were working alone), Hardt made a minor variation in the electrode-attachment procedure. During one and only one of the subsequent impedence tests, Hardt strongly focused his mind and directed the following suggestion to Alexander: "You will help us find friends to share this endeavor."

Within two seconds, Alexander suddenly moved, as if startled, opened his eyes, and asked if he had been pricked by something sharp. Alexander was assured that no one in the area had any sharp objects on hand and no physical invasion had been made. Both Hardt and his technical assistants were awed at Alexander's immediate and direct response to the nonverbal suggestion. Although this was a single test, it was the only time during seven days on which ten electrodes were attached that Alexander made such a response. In fact, it was the only response of its type out of 140 events noted.[12]

This left Hardt to wonder whether, since the communication was detected, it was also effective. Hardt waited six months to see if Alexander would respond to the telepathic suggestion. It was during this interval that Alexander introduced Foster

Gamble to Hardt, resulting in Foster and his wife, Dania, both completing the training. Hardt credited Alexander with providing this exciting contact. Gamble and Hardt, now working together on a permanent basis, have formed the Mind Center Corporation and are beginning to make advanced alpha enhancement training commercially available.

The advanced biofeedback training undertaken by Alexander and MacLachlan runs counter to conventional wisdom in the field of biofeedback. The National Research Council report of 1988 dismisses this research as unproductive, although it did not review Dr. Hardt's literature.

Clearly, the charts displayed in this chapter indicate the viability of alpha training, as well as a way to enhance collective thought through shared feedback. We believe this may be the next frontier for EEG training.

Alpha enhancement can benefit corporations and groups of people who must interact creatively on a continuing basis, as well as individuals, by reducing the time it takes for individuals to think productively and collectively.

For warriors—particularly those operating in small groups such as special-operations forces or high-level staffs, who must turn out coherent policy and plans—such training and the opportunity to think creatively together can enhance their ability to function and, ultimately, to survive.

11
THE ABSOLUTE WARRIOR

T he martial arts are the very foundation of the warrior's skills. Combat arts are as old as recorded history. The Gilgamesh epic praises its hero as a mighty warrior. The ancient year-kings, who ensured the harvest during prehistory, evolved into the seasonal warlords of antiquity; by the middle of the second millennium, B.C., these warlords had become year-round rulers. At the time of Moses, treaties were signed by kings describing themselves as "the Valiant," "the Hero," "Terrible in Battle." Homer's *Iliad* was partially a manual of combat tactics; our style of infantry battle is the direct descendant of Greek warfare, in which warriors massed for short-term confrontations designed to substitute for expensive wars of attrition. In all of these examples, personal valor and individual prowess won the day, the war—and in some cases, the kingdom.

Today, the martial arts are the most accessible introduction to an ancient practice, with us since prehistoric times. In the martial arts we meld our physical, mental, emotional, and spiritual selves. We learn to act as integrated beings, deriving self-consciousness and self-knowledge in the process. We become not only clear-headed and disciplined but possessors of the wisdom that mind-body integration brings.

To benefit from the martial arts, it may not be necessary to appreciate that we become, in the process, a link in history's chain. But consider: Alexander the Great carried the works of Homer with him into Asia. Plato talked of *skiamachia* ("fighting without an antagonist"), which survives in martial arts as shadow boxing. The martial arts teach oneness with universal forces; they bestow a sense of historical perspective, along with personal regard and increased competence.

Which art one chooses to follow is not as important as gaining a thorough understanding of the physical, mental, and even spiritual aspect of your chosen art. It is the total integration of all these aspects that provides the warrior with a basis for action. The student gains the physical skills necessary to meet and defeat any potential adversary, the wisdom to know when to engage in physical combat, and the restraint to apply only the force required to establish balance.

There are two major subdivisions of the martial arts: the hard arts, which require intense physical contact and force; and the soft arts, which emphasize movement and the application of a "universal" force called ki, or chi.

In the U.S., the most popular hard art may well be tae kwon do, a Korean form taught in the South and North Korean armies, and familiar to Americans from films and karate competitions. Tae kwon do emphasizes kata, the moving forms that teach correct positions, movements, skill, grace, and speed.

The aggressive hard arts are taught not only to American Special Forces but widely among the armed services. They are available to civilians through private instructors nationwide. In choosing a private instructor, look for an advanced instructor who understands and teaches the philosophy and true applications of tae kwon do, not merely the physical forms, since the benefits of forms without philosophy are limited.

To clarify the warrior spirit and sharpen your edge, we recommend a soft art such as aikido. Aikido philosophy blends body, mind, and spirit without teaching a single offensive move. In aikido, there are no pure sparring sessions and an injury to the partner reflects badly upon the thrower.

Aikido means a way to harmonize with the ki of the universe—to contact the universal force. Its founder, Morihei Ueshiba, describes it as "a loving attack and its peaceful solution."[1]

All martial arts presuppose a universal energy that flows through us. Acupuncture is based on this principle. So is tai chi, a discipline for developing *chi*, the life energy, without physical contact.

To contact and utilize this universal energy, the warrior utilizes four principles that are as valuable for confrontation in the boardroom as on the battlefield once their nature is understood.

THE FOUR PRINCIPLES

To unify the mind and body, you must adhere to four basic principles. First: the mind moves the body. Where your mind goes, your body will follow. Focus on the "one point," your body's center of gravity, approximately two inches below your navel. Moving from that point forward, backward, and side to side, you will maintain your balance and be very difficult to overcome. Some believe this one point is the origin of the individual's ki. By mentally concentrating ki in this point, you can become truly immovable. By keeping your consciousness centered in this area, you will be able to move freely and counter any attack—physical *or* mental.

Second: relax completely. The ability to relax the entire person allows us to unify the mind and the physical body, while drawing on the universal force to increase strength. Let the weight of the upper body settle to the "one point."[2]

Third: Keep weight underside. This means keeping the weight at the lowest point. Relax completely, using the one point, and this will occur naturally. By relaxing with the weight underside, you will gain great strength. For mental confrontations, this strength will be invaluable.

Fourth: Extend ki. Envision ki as coming from the one spot as a point of origin. This ki is an infinitely available, directable stream of energy that flows out of the body. While ki flows out, new ki can enter, keeping the body totally energized and healthy. A way to experience ki is to conduct a simple experiment known as the unbendable arm.[3]

THE UNBENDABLE ARM

To demonstrate the unbendable arm, one needs an assistant. First, extend your strongest arm, making it as tense as possible. Next, have your assistant pull down on it with enough force to lower the arm. Resist hard. Your arm still comes down relatively easily. Now extend the arm again and project ki by imagining your arm as a fire hose with water flowing through it. Mentally, raise the ki from your one point so it flows through your arm and out to a distant point—as far as a hundred, a thousand, or a million miles away. Imagine the ki rushing from your one spot, where it is infinitely available, up through your arm, and out to this distant location. The arm is itself relatively relaxed; it is not tensed by muscles. Have your assistant pull down on the arm while you are concentrating on projecting ki to the distant point. The assistant will notice how much more difficult it is to pull down the arm when your ki is flowing. As the ki is flowing, the arm becomes unbendable. This easy exercise allows you to begin controlling ki.[4]

To project ki, as in learning any martial art, familiarize yourself with your body. Learn your arousal levels before trying advanced body-mind-integration techniques. These techniques stem from total harmony. They are not just rehearsed physical moves. A true master is in total harmony when performing his art. He or she is never hurried and is not thinking of the routine. The master *is* the routine. They are one.

GROUNDING

Using your one point, you can become *grounded*. By this we mean sending the ki down into the earth so you always remain balanced. All martial arts require that you remain centered and balanced. It is your balance that allows you to overcome any aggressor, whether in the field or the conference room. This grounding can make you literally immovable, mentally or physically.

Grounding can be very useful in business or in daily life. It is helpful to be grounded during social interactions, especially if you are uneasy because of a new situation or large crowd of strangers. You will find yourself dealing with others more effectively when you have a sense of being in balance.

You may remember making a presentation and being unsure of its reception. Do you remember how you felt before you went in and while you were speaking? Being uncertain of yourself is a form of being out of balance.

There will always be times when you are unsure of the outcome. By being centered and balanced, mentally and physically, you can prepare yourself to deal with any eventuality.

One simple method of becoming balanced is to project ki all around you, in contact with the ground. Hold your one point. Keep your weight underside. These techniques help both with physical and mental balance.

A technique some use to get in contact with the ground or floor is to stamp their feet. This helps give you a sense of being centered. Use this approach when you feel mentally off balance and want quick reassurance.[5]

Another practical use of ki in daily life is handy for mothers in calming small children: Using a simple creative visualization technique, a mother can guide a child through a game of "dropping your monkey's tail." This involves guided imagery: having the child imagine he or she is a monkey with a long, thin tail. The monkey then tries to make its tail touch the ground. In so doing, make the child "believe" he or she really has a tail and that when the tail touches the ground, it will feel really good.

This affects the ki force by directing an umbilical cord to the earth and gently "grounding out" the child, who'll then be more calm and may even fall asleep.

The way of the universe is a way of remaining in balance and in harmony with nature. This moving *with*, not against, energy opens the mind's creative paths. These principles are universal and apply throughout life, bringing us to the realization we are *one* with the universe, totally integrated in mind, body, and spirit.

MORE BREATHING EXERCISES

Breathing exercises play an important part in all military training, even, as we have seen, in marksmanship. Not all martial-arts trainers fully emphasize breathing exercises, a vital training process. We recommend choosing an art form with heavy emphasis on breathing.

To practice breathing for martial arts, begin in a kneeling position. Place your feet close together. Have your knees about two fist-widths apart. Start with your back straight and your hands resting on your thighs. Exhale slowly. Lean slightly forward and expel any remaining air. This exhalation should take twenty to thirty seconds.

Pause a second or two. Now inhale slowly, until it seems you have completely filled your lungs; then add just a bit more. When inhaling for a period such as twenty or thirty seconds, think of the air traveling down to your one point and revitalizing ki. Fill the lower abdomen and the areas under your shoulder blades while thinking of the flow of ki throughout your body.

Through these breathing exercises, you are learning to control ki. As you exhale, visualize ki projecting to a distant place. While inhaling, visualize new ki flowing in to renew and sustain you.

Once you have established a breathing control pattern, you can conduct the exercises while you drive or while stuck in traffic. By holding your one point while doing breathing exercise, you will stay calm while maintaining the alertness necessary for driving a car in traffic. Practice during meetings, when walking, or at almost any other time. The important point is to practice breathing during varied, sometimes stressful, circumstances.

One of the early American experts in Japanese karate was Henry Slomanski. While a U.S. Army master sergeant in Japan shortly after World War II, Slomanski had the unusual assignment of hangman when the Japanese war criminals were being convicted and executed. Slomanski, during his years in Japan, learned the Japanese form of karate, rising to very high ranks. At one time he was considered third in the world, a feat not accomplished by any other Westerner. In addition to the physical arts, breathing, and mental training, he spent two years learning activities such as flower arranging and painting. This seemed very strange to a Westerner at first, but he later came to understand the mental discipline required and the relationship to the martial arts themselves.[6]

Such mental discipline becomes extremely important when being attacked. One must not become angry, for anger is the result of the mind's wandering from the one point. By focusing on your one point during the attack, you will optimize your response, mentally and physically.

This concept of maintaining mental discipline and not stooping to anger is crucial in warfighting. In a *60 Minutes* interview, Morley Safer talked with a soldier who had fought against the Americans in Vietnam. This soldier described being bombed on the Ho Chi Minh Trail by U.S. B-52s. Safer asked if the use of such intense force against him hadn't made him very angry. The soldier responded that it had not and that they would have lost everything had they allowed themselves to be angry.[7]

There are other benefits to the development of ki. Those who have worked in the field suggest it can be very beneficial to the maintenance of health. A demonstration of health-related ki can be seen in the annual ritual that occurs during the first three days of each Chinese new year. Koichi Tohei, a disciple of Professor Ueshiba, tells of going to the mountains, where the

The Absolute Warrior

temperature is in the low teens. During this period, a group gets together and actually enters the mountain rivers, even though the water is extremely cold. They accomplish this by mentally preparing themselves, maintaining their center or one point, and projecting ki. They find they are able to do this and stay in the water for several minutes at a time, although it is barely above the freezing temperature. This is not a matter of ignoring the cold but of having the body and mind totally integrated.[8]

A similar application was mentioned by Chaplain Grady Spry. Chaplain Spry was assigned to a unit of the 25th Infantry Division, which was deployed to South New Zealand during its winter, when the weather is very cold. Chaplain Spry had recently attended a lecture by Tohei and had heard the story of how to keep warm during cold periods. Applying Tohei's techniques, although dressed relatively lightly, Spry was able to keep warm for long periods of time while others, who were heavily clothed, suffered.[9]

John Alexander attended a conference where, under Tohei's direction, two individuals got down on their hands and knees and Alexander was made to lie down, face up, with his legs and shoulders resting on the two individuals' backs. Tohei then instructed Alexander to just remain still and allow the ki to flow, while three very large men then sat on Alexander's stomach. The suggestion that ki was running through Alexander allowed him to remain strong during this feat. During the same conference, although Alexander had extensive experience in both tae kwon do and shotokan karate, he was thrown by the Japanese gentleman with a simple movement of the hand that mentally projected ki. A slight movement of the wrist, of no more than two inches, then drove Alexander to the ground—not through a forceful strike, but because of the ki involved.

While in Hawaii, Alexander came into contact with Richard Haake, who was raised on Maui, where his father was a police captain and aikido was the martial art taught to the entire police force. Rich Haake, a black belt at an early age, mentioned very advanced aikido tests that seem phenomenal by normal standards. In one test, using a sword, the practitioner mentally holds running water still enough to pass the blade through the stopped water without wetting the sword. Another test involves using a round bamboo stick to slice rice paper: done incorrectly, the rice paper will tear into very jagged pieces; using ki to precede the stick, the result is a razor-sharp cut.[10]

In listening to these phenomenal cases, a correlation arises between the application of ki and the use of PK, or psychokinesis. To explore this correlation, Alexander and others briefly studied under Guy Savelli, a practitioner of kun tao karate. Savelli, who suggests that this form employs psychokinesis as a primary energy source, has been tested by several laboratories, and some anecdotal evidence supports his conjecture.[11]

What was unique to Savelli's training was the speed with which one progressed: Within a period of three days, members of the group were able to break boards with a flick of the wrist, puncture fruit with a finger, and even, in one case, have a metal bar bent across the individual's chest. Savelli suggests that these feats are accomplished not through physical force but rather via the development of ki, or psychokinetic force projected beyond the body.

One of the first group exercises began with Savelli striking a fairly substantial blow to each person's chest. It was up to the individual to move *prior* to the blow landing, by mentally intercepting a command to strike before the physical strike began. If one waited until the movement began, it was too late to get out of the way.

Try this in relative safety by having an individual willing to deliver *a noninjurious blow*. Be sure *you* are willing to accept the blow delivered if you engage in this exercise. Have the person doing the striking telegraph the blow mentally, not by squinting or any physical movement prior to the strike. You will find, in a very short period of time, that you are able to perceive when the strike will occur and begin moving away prior to that instant.

This practice is similar to the training of the ancient samurai.

Samurai from opposing clans reportedly could encounter each other and know whether or not the rival was intent on attacking once he had passed. To survive, one had to be able to perceive the attack before it was initiated.

Breaking of one-inch pine boards is relatively easy, as we have mentioned. This board breaking was done not with the fist but with a blow from the back of an open hand, the actual striking force coming from one or two fingers hitting the board. This indicates sufficient psychokinetic energy preceding the hand to allow the strike to break the board.

To train for such board breaking, we exercised using mouse-traps. A loaded mousetrap was set at exactly an arm's length from the individual. Trainees tried to flick the wrist fast enough to set off the mousetrap and recoil the striking finger before the trap closed. We recommend a very light mousetrap if you plan to try this technique. The consequences of failure with heavy traps are significant.

Before using the traps themselves, practice flicking your wrists and aiming. Once you can project energy and move with the required degree of speed, you may use the same technique to break boards safely enough. Do not smash through the board. Rather, attack it with a flick of the wrist. Pull back almost at the same instant you initially touch the board.

Another training technique is the puncturing of an orange. This may sound fairly simple, but pick up an orange and try sticking your finger into it. The flexibility of the orange gives it considerable strength. Now place two or three fingers closely together and, again, using psychokinesis or ki, *project* the fingers through the fruit. Strike very quickly, with the mind projecting force ahead of the strike.

Savelli also teaches the ability to attack an opponent by interrupting his or her mental processes. He calls the technique "The Mind Stops." This is an advanced technique in which the mind of the opponent is blocked and he is unable to effectively strike you.

Savelli says this is the technique he would employ if faced

with an attacker holding a gun. Others confirmed seeing a gun-wielding opponent remain still while Savelli maneuvered behind him. The attacker reported seeing nothing from the time Savelli was in front of him until Savelli struck the attacker from behind.

Similar stories appear in Soviet literature. Joseph Stalin, who had a known interest in psychic phenomena, had a famous psychic, Wolf Messing, brought in to demonstrate his reputed capabilities. Messing was invited by Stalin to try entering the heavily guarded Kremlin without being caught. Reportedly, Messing walked undetected by numerous guards, all of whom appeared conscious and alert. Messing claimed he could cloud people's minds, thereby becoming virtually invisible. [12]

To begin developing exceptional mental control, learn to extinguish a candle using only concentration. To practice, place a lighted candle eight to ten feet from you, far enough to prevent you from accidentally blowing out the candle when exhaling. Remember, you wish to *mentally* extinguish the candle, not create air currents that put it out.

Next, mentally focus your energy on your objective. Think of energy projecting from your eyes. Visualize the flame becoming smaller and smaller. Stare intently at the flame. When so intently focused, you may not be aware of external surroundings or events. Continue to hold your concentration as long as possible.

In time, the candle should become dimmer and go out. This is an advanced skill that requires practice to accomplish. This exercise should be attempted only after learning the mind-calming techniques and gaining a degree of control over your mental processes.

In working with Savelli, we saw evidence of dim mak, also known as the quivering palm or death touch. In the lore of the martial arts, dim mak is said to be a way to strike, interrupting ki, that leads to the victim's death a few hours later. The fabled death touch does not kill instantaneously, nor is it administered using great physical force.

The force applied, reportedly relatively light, sets up a vibration that interrupts ki. The individual continues to live for some time and then suddenly dies a few hours later. The degree of time delay, according to the lore, is controlled by the choice of strike zone, strike, and time of delivery.

The evidence Savelli presented to support the existence of dim mak was in the form of tests done on two goats. Savelli himself applied the strikes. The goats were then observed constantly for the next few hours. At the twelve-hour period, one of the goats dropped dead. The second one died approximately twenty-four hours after being struck. An autopsy was done on the goats to determine cause of death. In both goats autopsied, the hearts had spontaneously stopped pumping. Both hearts were full of blood, as if they had not even contracted at the time of death. Inside each animal's chest was an energy path that looked like an exit wound from a bullet or other sharp projectile. However, no entrance wound was found. There was no massive bleeding or damage at the point where the strike had occurred on either animal. This was the first time, to our knowledge, that dim mak was applied and observed, followed by autopsies to determine the actual causes of death.

The martial arts offer a great range of possibilities, because the energy applied is neutral. How we use it is the important factor. True martial-arts masters and great warriors alike understand the responsibility that goes with learning these arts. It is the way of the warrior monk, a way of integrating mind, body, and spirit. Ki, or chi, may be used either to harm or defend, and may also assist in maintaining health. We recommend that you use these latter modes—for defense if absolutely necessary, and for health and the betterment of the world whenever possible.

12

SELF-TESTS: PUSHING THE ENVELOPE OF HUMAN PERFORMANCE

Thus far, we have explored simple methods of controlling the mind and body and influencing human performance. To broaden our understanding of reality's malleability, we experimented with techniques of modeling, visualization, and remote viewing. In so doing, we have seen the human being as an integrated unit of body, mind, and spirit. In this final adventure, we intend to "push the envelope" of your beliefs even more.

Pushing the envelope, an aviation term, means stretching an aircraft's performance to its upper limits—seeing how fast or far it will fly, learning how much stress the airframe or engine can endure. Pushing the envelope of belief means expanding horizons of possibility.

To act effectively, the warrior must be able to expand beliefs to encompass new possibilities. By testing those possibilities personally, the warrior determines whether they offer an advantage—and if securing that advantage is worth the risk. The possibilities we use here to push reality's envelope are not risk free.

Self-Tests: Pushing the Envelope of Human Performance

PSYCHOKINESIS

Psychokinesis, or mind over matter, is a phenomenon as old as man's self-awareness. We mentioned martial-arts practitioners who believe that they tap psychokinetic energy to strike their targets. Now we will teach you how to test this possibility.

To discuss psychokinesis, or PK, in terms of the observable, physical world, we will break it into two subsets: macro-PK and micro-PK.

Macro-PK refers to events where visible deformation of gross metal objects occurs, or where an object of substance is moved without the application of normal physical means or force. Macro-PK events are easily observable with the naked eye, without instrumentation.

Micro-PK, in contrast, occurs in ways that require scientific instrumentation to detect. You cannot see micro-PK events occur, but you can see the results, such as changes in a random-event generator (REG), when displayed on a statistical basis. Micro-PK also creates very small physical effects (deformation, annealing, heating, or other changes) within a metal structure at a microscopic level.

At the Princeton Engineering Anomalies Research (PEAR) Laboratory, Dr. Robert Jahn, Brenda Dunne, and others are using various instruments, including cascade and random-event generators, to show that micro-PK effects are quantifiable.[1]

If you walked into a PEAR laboratory while a micro-PK experiment was taking place, you might see a human trying to mentally affect the distribution of a number of cascading balls, not unlike the random cascade of balls in any state lottery.

The PEAR experiments, of course, are not confined to any one medium or type of experimentation, and the individual effects documented tend to be very small. These effects observed at PEAR are, however, statistically significant, repeatable, and transferable from one medium to another.

Because PEAR research concentrates on reliable, human-generated micro-PK effects that can occur in engineering systems such as computers, the significance of this research to government and industry is undeniable. Micro-PK effects can seemingly alter the performance of a bit of information in a complex system. If that system is a missile-guidance system or a computer network or a satellite telemetry package, then the results may be much greater than the micro-PK effect itself.

Do the micro-PK effects seen in random-event generator experiments represent the ability of the human mind to affect probability itself? Or do they merely shape a desired result on a one-time basis by causing a greater percentage of balls to fall in a particular pattern than chance would predict? PEAR's work represents the most sustained and thorough attempt in modern times to come up with a description of reality that includes the effect of mind on man's world.

The PEAR data from Princeton is especially impressive in its consistency: There are now over a billion established data points in the studies.[2] Even Carl Sagan, a founding member of CSICOP (Committee for Scientific Investigation of Claims of the Paranormal), after attending Dr. Jahn's presentation at Cornell University in July 1988, stated that he was impressed by the data, and suggested that PEAR's model should be employed by parapsychologists in order to validate their results.[3]

In 1983, then Lieutenaut-Colonel John Alexander met with Julian Isaacs, at that time a doctoral candidate working on sophisticated micro-PK experimentation, at Cambridge University in England. Although Isaacs had frequently observed macro-PK metal-bending events, his experiments were designed to demonstrate micro-PK using piezo-electric crystal, which gives off a very slight electrical signal when stressed.

During his visit, Alexander had the opportunity to observe and experiment with the system Isaacs was using to demonstrate micro-PK on a piezo-electric crystal target. During experiments, Isaacs had found that a human subject could cause an electrical response to register in the monitored laboratory environment.

To ensure that only the designated target was affected, and to prove that only the desired target was generating any resultant

Self-Tests: Pushing the Envelope of Human Performance

signal, Isaacs installed a second, control, crystal to monitor the natural environment. If both crystals registered a signal, then the micro-PK event could be discounted due to a spurious electrical impulse.

Isaacs's results repeatedly demonstrated that the target crystal could be influenced to generate a signal on command. To further substantiate that claim, Isaacs would let the system run for hours in an unattended mode, thus showing that the micro-PK events happened only when intended. The effect was proven not to be caused by external stimuli such as physical shaking or electromagnetic flux in the area.

Alexander came away convinced and intrigued, after working with the system. What Isaacs seemed to have found was a trainable skill with an inherent learning curve. Subjects initially had "beginner's luck" (or novice effect) with the system, followed by a tapering off of prowess. After several subsequent sessions, the subject learned to identify and control the effect, and the percentage of micro-PK hits increased dramatically. These results imply that psychokinesis can be learned.

Machines put together by Ed Kelley and Ross Dunseath at Duke University[4] followed Isaacs's model but are capable of isolating the target crystal from vibration, which could cause an accidental event. They installed an EEG to monitor the subject attempting to affect the target without touching it.

If a target can be affected in this fashion—from a distance, without physical tampering—the military and security applications are of great importance. There are major implications if micro-PK can be controlled. When questioned on this matter at a conference, Dr. Jahn stated that he thought the greatest danger lay in micro-electronics such as the subsystems found in high-performance aircraft. Dr. Robert Morris has published studies on the impact of micro-PK on computers.

John Alexander says, "It is certainly my view that the greatest threat in the application of micro-PK is to attack computers. The systems do not need to be incapacitated; they only need to be made unreliable."

Through these instrumented approaches to micro-PK, we have begun to demonstrate repeatable results. We are formulating theories of how and why such events occur. The lack of an established theoretical base has long been a stumbling block for scientists, because many recorded events run counter to what should occur according to classical physics. Traditionally, this sort of dichotomy leads to a revision of theory, not of history.

Macro-PK

A Macro-PK experience can change belief systems. Macro-PK events are tangible, require minimal equipment to perform, and usually leave the subject with a memento of the event: a bent spoon, a stopped clock, and the knowledge that something incontrovertible *happened*.

The fact that people who have experienced macro-PK revise their belief systems is, in itself, a tangible result.

Historically, macro-PK research has been done with a gifted subject, such as Uri Geller, demonstrating. Researchers observed the events to determine what occurred, then attempted to validate their observations and formulate a theoretical construct to explain the events.

Jack Houck, an aerospace engineer, originated the protocols for the PK "party."[5] Since 1981, these PK parties have allowed thousands of people to perform psychokinesis for themselves. You can too. But before you invite your friends over to try macro-PK, let us tell you how to throw a PK party.

The host, acting as the instructor, shows the group inexpensive forks and spoons while he discusses PK briefly, explaining the scientific background. This helps encourage participants to believe that ordinary people can produce macro-PK effects.

The instructor places the forks and spoons within reach and the participants are asked to touch or "sense" them, while searching for a piece that subjectively "feels" best. Upon receiving a positive response, each picks up a fork or spoon and finds a comfortable seat. The instructor asks them to close their eyes, relax, and take a deep breath.

The instructor asks the group to visualize, or mentally form, a huge ball of energy. This energy is external and is infinitely available. You may choose to see it, hear it, or feel it, depending on your favorite representational system. Most Americans tend to visualize a huge ball of white energy.

The instructor has the participants condense this ball of energy, making it ever more intense. Participants are told to keep their eyes closed and to visualize the ball of energy coming down to the forehead. Then, each mentally moves the ball of energy into the body, while the instructor directs it down through their hands and into their forks or spoons.

The instructor leads the group in saying, "Bend, bend, bend."

Saying "bend," three times imbues the event with the group's intention. Once the command is verbalized, the subjects open their eyes and rub the palms of their hands, or their thumbs and forefingers, over the necks of their forks or spoons. When a change in the temperature or hardness of the metal is noticed, the subject takes two hands—one on top and one on the bottom of the implement—and presses slightly. The implement will bend over rather easily.

Do not be afraid to apply some physical force. The important thing is to recognize the subjective state-change when it takes place and to catalog that response. Note what is going on mentally, physically, and emotionally when you feel the spoon or fork soften.

As soon as the first person is successful, that person should tell the others that a macro-PK event has occurred. We have found a synergistic response associated with individual success. Jack Houck suggests that such success creates a peak emotional response, and he recommends that subjects try to generate enthusiasm, which seems to have a positive influence on the occurrence of macro-PK events.

At PK parties, it is not uncommon to have 90 to 100 percent of the people demonstrating success with this sort of macro-PK.

About an hour into the party, once the entire set of instructions has been run a few times and the participants are satisfied with the group's metal-bending skills, the instructor tells the group it is time to do PK without any force being applied.

The instructor should have pairs of matched forks—forks that come from the same set. Before beginning the exercise, everyone should examine these forks.

Fit them together and notice how snugly they lie. Do this in pairs, with each fork of the pair in front, in case there is a significant difference in the shape of one fork or minor bending of certain tines. In order to catalog later changes in the forks, you must know the starting positions of the tines and how well the forks matched.

Once all have examined the forks, whoever has matched sets takes one fork in each hand, holding the very base of the fork.

The instructor tells the participants that they may not touch the tines from this point on in the experiment, and then repeats the preparatory steps of the earlier exercise: helping the participants create the energy, condense it, move it through the arm, and into the fork.

Again, the instructor leads the group in saying, "Bend, bend, bend." This vocalization is a critical step that catalyzes the bending process. Whenever someone sees actual bending, the others should be encouraged to watch. In this format, spontaneous metal bending occurs approximately 5 percent of the time, although the percentage varies from group to group.

The composition of the group may also impact its success. The least fruitful sessions have been those where scientists are participating in front of disbelieving peers, on their own turf where their credibility may be at risk. The most fruitful sessions often include children, whose belief systems are less rigid than many adults', or adults who have had training in meditation, martial arts, or other mind-expanding disciplines.

John Alexander was first introduced to Jack Houck, the innovator of the PK party, in 1982.[6] After experiencing metal bending at one of Houck's parties, Alexander offered to host a PK party at his own apartment.

Two months later, the party took place at Alexander's apartment. The guest list was comprised of people from the military and intelligence community, such as Major General Stubblebine, who were interested in the potential of PK as a military and intelligence tool. Also attending were paranormal researchers, including Ann Gehman, a well-known psychic.

During the first phase of the party, conducted in accordance with the directions we have given you, a number of people experienced significant bending. During the second phase of the session, while attempting PK without applying physical force, Ann Gehman was one of those who held a pair of forks by their base.

Initially, she tried to stare down the forks, never a successful strategy, and had no success. Suddenly something distracted her and then, in full view of onlookers, one of her forks bent. The tines and neck of the fork drooped a full 90 degrees.

Both Alexander and Stubblebine, who saw the event and were certain that no physical force had bent the fork, agreed that the potential of this phenomenon warranted further research.[7]

PK parties have trained hundreds of people, including many top military, intelligence, and elected government officials. John Marsh, former secretary of the army, has been briefed on the results of these PK parties.

The security implications of macro-PK, if it can be learned and controlled, are far-reaching. Militarily, weapons systems could be made not to function on schedule, or to malfunction when necessary.

The Soviets as well are exploring applied psychokinesis, as a number of published articles confirm. Larissa Vilenskaya brought pictures to the West of applied psychokinesis in Soviet-directed research. These pictures show people apparently levitating and moving objects psychokinetically.[8]

The U.S. Defense Intelligence Agency compiled a report on

Soviet efforts in mind control and controlled offensive behavior.[9] The report suggests continuing research of the sort in which Nina Kulagina, famed Soviet psychic, claimed to stop a frog's heart from beating.

The Czechoslovakian scientist Robert Pavlita reported working on psychotronic devices designed to concentrate and direct psychic energy sufficiently to kill test organisms.[10]

Such reports spur American interest. Senator Claiborne Pell, in 1989, called for the U.S. government to sponsor further research into human capabilities.

Ed Speakman, a government science adviser and inventor of the car antenna, was at a PK party attended by many government professionals and sitting three feet away from one of the participants when a fork "spontaneously" bent. As everyone cried out that the fork had bent, the fork—still without any physical force being applied—came back to its original position, drooped again to a 90-degree bend, and finally settled at a 45-degree bend.

Enough of these spontaneous PK events have been observed to convince us that some process is at work here that, if harnessed, could impact national security.

Significant analytical scientific work has been done to validate macro-PK events. In the mid-1970s, Professor John Hasted, a physicist at Birbeck College, University of London, reported on children bending metal by paranormal means while the metal objects were sealed in glass containers.[11]

Scanning electron microscopes have been used to examine the difference between forks bent by macro-PK and those bent by physical force. At extreme magnification, the appearance of PK-bent metal and force-bent metal varies widely. Studies in the United States and Japan using photo-microscopy also clearly show this difference between PK-bent metal and metal bent by physical force.[12]

John Alexander's photo (figure 5) of a hacksaw blade rolled up in a 360-degree circle using PK is remarkable because a hacksaw blade is so brittle that it will frequently snap if bent, even slightly, using physical force. In 1982, between September 15 and November 19, Houck and Dahlen brought hacksaw blades wrapped in a bag to three PK parties and left the bag under participants' chairs, never once targeting the blades. During these exposures to ambient PK only, the Rockwell hardness of the blades inside the bag lessened progressively. (See figure 6.) A control blade, never brought to the parties, remained at the same Rockwell hardness throughout the experimental period.[13]

If such softening force were to be applied over time to crucial aircraft components or other military objectives, the results could be catastrophic. Further study may allow us to harness and understand these forces.

Some suggest that there is a connection between PK and the healing of wounds. If so, this is an expression of the interaction between consciousness and matter.

As in the case of remote-viewing phenomena, micro- and macro-PK effects may seem anomalous only because our understanding of the physical world 'is incomplete. If enough people experience macro-PK effects personally, following the simple protocols we offer, a consensus may develop that will support large-scale research at the unclassified level.

FIRE WALKING

The term *trial by fire* has historically symbolized an individual's passage into true warriorship. Although the modern warrior need not walk on a bed of hot coals to prove himself, some still do.

Why? To demonstrate that mastery over mind and body is complete. We must warn you: Fire walking should only be attempted under the tutelage of an experienced instructor. People have been seriously burned attempting it. In some cases, unprepared individuals have died from fire walking. And we must emphasize that we are not implying or suggesting that a test of fire is necessary to true warriorship. *If you decide to fire walk, proceed with caution and under supervision.*

Fire walking is still practiced in ceremonies in Brazil, Burma,

Figure #5

Hacksaw Blades Bent by PK

Note: Some physical force was applied. However, hacksaw blades are very brittle and usually snap if twisted or bent. PHOTO BY JOHN ALEXANDER

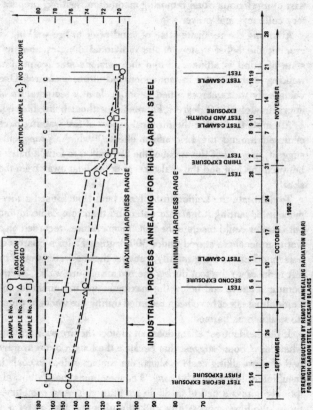

Figure #6

THIS CHART FIRST APPEARED IN *A CONCEPTUAL MODEL OF PARANORMAL PHENOMENA, INFORMATION TRANSFER AND BRAIN-MIND INTERACTION* BY JACK HOUK.

Bulgaria, Fiji, Greece, Japan, Tahiti, Spain, Sri Lanka, Malaysia, and—recently—here in the United States. It is often part of a religious ritual requiring meditation, fasting, preparatory celibacy, and prayer.

Attaining the requisite state of mind prior to fire walking is crucial; the belief system of the individual dictates how that state of mind is attained. From the warrior's standpoint, fire walking is an exercise in motivation and ultimate control: One voluntarily walks across a bed of hot coals at a temperature of approximately 1300 degrees Fahrenheit without being burned.

Attempts to devalue the mystical aspect of fire walking have centered around the Leidenfrost effect,[14] which, proponents suggest, may cause the sweat of the fire walker to form a barrier between the foot and the coals, keeping the heat away from the skin.

To calibrate the Leidenfrost effect, Jack Houck used a thermocouple, putting it first into water and then into flame to find out if water could insulate the foot. Temperatures recorded on a wet thermocouple stayed under 300 degrees F. for a quarter of a second before rising rapidly, proving that no water would be left to insulate the foot during the remaining fire walk.[15] Temperatures above and below the maximum and minimum for the Leidenfrost effect have been recorded during fire walks in which no walker was harmed.[16]

If the Leidenfrost effect does not protect the fire walker, then what does? Some suggest that because the length of an average bed of fire-walking coals is short, the contact of foot to coals is insufficient to produce burning. Yet sometimes those who walk quickly across a bed of coals do get burned.[17] And sometimes those who have successfully walked during one session burn at subsequent sessions.[18]

Some walkers have chosen to stand for as long as seven seconds on hot stones with a recorded temperature of up to 600 degrees F.[19] When heat-sensitive paint was applied to the soles of a stone walker's feet, the paint indicated that the feet never exceeded 150 degrees F., far below the rock temperature.

Self-Tests: Pushing the Envelope of Human Performance

Somehow, practitioners hold all potential burning effects in abeyance. *Successful fire walkers agree that attaining and maintaining the proper mental state is the key to crossing the fire unharmed.*

Animal tissue, when heated above 140 degrees, normally exhibits surface burns. Fire walkers, through mental control over physiological processes, create in themselves a short-term fire immunity.

To investigate this phenomenon, John Alexander participated in a day of warrior's-edge exercises that began in the morning with martial-arts modeling; it continued, in the afternoon, with PK metal bending and concluded, in the evening, with fire walking.

Approximately twenty people, including Alexander, underwent the entire course, including fire walking. All of them were interested in exploring the possible limits of human excellence modeling. The military officers in the group were particularly concerned with using motivation as a tool to overcome fear.

Outside Annapolis, Maryland, on a small farm, while the hot coals were being readied, the group prepared mentally by evaluating fear. They discussed things that frightened them. Someone suggested that knowledge was an antidote to fear: To reduce fear, one first must identify the fear; then analyze it in detail; and finally, accept the consequences of overcoming it, since the mind uses fear to prevent the body from acting.

For three hours, the group watched the fire burn down and prepared themselves, using an NLP model to evaluate physiological change and anchor desired states.

Then finally, the instructor determined that it was time to attempt the fire walk.

This fire was of hardwood, raked into a pattern four feet wide by twelve feet long. Around it, the instructor gathered the group, asking who would choose to walk the fire. A low-light television camera was ready to record the event.

Even then, no individual was expected to walk the fire who was not confident of his ability to do so unharmed. Each walker had to believe he had achieved the appropriate mental and physical states to walk. Three people declined to walk and moved away to watch.

The instructor first stood in front of the fire quietly and then slowly began walking across the hardwood coals. Once he was across, the remaining seventeen, one at a time, crossed the fire.

Alexander likened the physiological state he experienced to the excitement during critical football or basketball games. Focusing his attention upward, off the fire, he repeated mentally, "cool moss," as his feet touched the hardwood coals.

Once the walkers had crossed the fire, the instructor evaluated the physical and mental state of each. Some chose to make a second trip across the coals. In one case, the instructor stopped a person and worked privately with the walker for several minutes before releasing him to cross the fire safely.

Of the seventeen who walked that fire, with a pyrometer reading of approximately 1300 degrees F., none sustained so much as a single blister on the foot.

With the television camera still rolling, several walkers then sat or squatted around the fire and picked up red-hot coals, holding them for two or three seconds without ill effect.

Because any warrior must control reactions to fear, this firewalking experience was invaluable to the participants. Leaders of soldiers and trainers of warriors must understand this process at a gut level, in order to evaluate human-potential programs. Fear is a prime driver in modern society; it must be managed. It cannot be ignored.

In Julianne Blake's "Attribution of Power in Transformation of Fear: An Empirical Study of Firewalking,"[20] the clinical psychologist looked at those who did, and did not, blister during fire walks. One hundred percent of the nonblisterers reported that they could re-create the enabling state in which they successfully walked on fire.

This agrees with worldwide anecdotal data supporting the premise that a specific, identifiable mental state is at the heart of successful fire walking.

Fire walking will change your belief system at an experiential level. Your belief-system tree, from its roots to its highest branches, is nurtured by experience. The experience of fire walking is immediately transferable into one's life. As with macro-PK metal bending, it expands the possibilities that your belief system can encompass. If you can walk on fire, what else can you do that you once thought impossible?

The military is concerned with quickly motivating people to do things that are inherently dangerous to them. While sitting around the fire after Alexander and others had walked it, someone asked, "What would it be like to have battalions of troops, trained with this capability, ready to go into combat?"

And someone replied, "You wouldn't have to send them into combat—just tell the enemy they're coming."

For the individual warrior, fire walking offers great potential. It allows you to overcome one of humanity's most innate fears. To walk on fire requires absolute control of the mind as well as a belief system empowered by the human will.

This is not something for everyone. But for the ultimate warrior, it provides the opportunity to overcome fear and opens up untold possibilities in the realm of reality mapping.

THE BEST DEFENSE . . .

Some say that the best defense is a strong offense. Some say that the best defense is to be prepared for any eventuality.

The world around us is changing with increasing speed, partly due to the speed of information transfer itself. Such concepts as situational ethics, which undermine the shared morality of civilized people, complicate the task of deciding what is aggression and what is simply confusion.

We think that information is your best defense against confusion, against being overwhelmed by the changes barraging us continuously from all over the world.

We have given you the information we think will best serve to make you an active, not reactive, participant in life. We are offering not the antidote to change but the ability to change yourself to accommodate all changes. We humbly suggest that human excellence is the best defense against human error, human failing, and human aggression.

The warrior learns on the battlefield how to survive by adapting. We have given you the tools to adapt your belief system, integrate your mind and body, expand your reality map, and use your success space to become not only the best that you can be but the best you can imagine that anyone can be.

Many people today live lives so decoupled and compartmentalized that their experience, mostly vicarious, is virtually acquired in a closet. These people can be dangerous precisely because so little has actually happened to them that they cannot comprehend and do not weigh the effect of their actions on others. Yet these closet people seldom mean anyone harm and their exile is easily ended. To break free, they must only open the closet door and step out into the world.

When encountering such people, the warrior defends himself first with patience, then with cleverness, and only last with as little force as possible. Remember: The superior man fights only great battles.

Because the warrior learns self-respect and respect for others in combat, where life may depend on the goodwill of your friends and the respect of your enemies, the warrior approaches potential confrontations cautiously. The warrior behaves with respect toward all beings and with an honor code sometimes difficult to teach those whose lives have never been on the line.

We have tried to teach you that code, or at least a respect for it, as we have led you through the various doors of self-optimization.

A friend of ours has above her desk an unattributed quote: "If not me, then who? If now now, then when?" We remind you now that you can do no better in life for yourself and others than you expect. We have tried to teach you that expectation breeds result and that most of your undertakings are subject to self-imposed limitations. Similarly, the need to defend oneself is often a matter of interpretation.

Self-Tests: Pushing the Envelope of Human Performance

We would be proud and happy if the warrior's edge—the warrior's respect for life and devotion to duty, the warrior's uprightness, the warrior's determination to excel—spread through the population and made the world a better place to live and one in which defense from aggression was unnecessary. Since humans evolve at different rates and with conflicting goals, this is unlikely to happen anytime soon.

So we will be content with having given it our collective best shot. The warrior meets his own standard. One of our aims was to give any reader the tools to become better at work and play. We think we have done that. We know these techniques work. We also know that no medicine is effective if it is left in its bottle instead of being swallowed by the patient.

You can now use more of your mind and more of your body in an integrated fashion. You can take advantage of your physiological connection with the ordering force of the universe to become strong, to shape your future, to gain your heart's desire.

What you *will* do is in no way predicated on what you *can* do. Unfortunately, we cannot stop you from using these techniques to oppress your fellow, to achieve selfish ends at the expense of your society and the biosphere, or to become the worst that you can be.

The warrior's edge itself was developed over centuries to counter just such threats to humanity's desire to live in peace.

Given that some will make effective use of these techniques without having learned the good judgment that years of training and risk instill, you may need to defend yourself against such people.

Defense through belief systems consists of truly believing that one is indomitable. Some of our greatest warriors and statesmen have survived and prospered using this basic shield of belief. If you believe that what you are doing is right, if you believe that you are healthy, happy, prosperous, and lucky—that you deserve only success—then you are in some ways protected already. Use your belief-system tree not only to reach for the sky but to root yourself firmly in the soil of right action.

Defense through quieting the mind is defense against the errors of misjudgment that come from confusion and precipitous action. Take a moment, when confronted with crises, to quiet your mind. That moment will be cheaply spent if it saves hours, days, weeks, or years of subsequent damage control and the regret that follows the exercise of poor judgment.

Defense through influence is defense through intervention. All intelligence techniques require ruthlessness, duplicity, and absolute integrity. No, these are not contradictions in terms. If you are using influence technologies correctly, you can and will achieve your objective by the manipulation of others. Recognize what you are doing; we do. If this manipulation is for the eventual benefit of these others as well as yourself, then you are adhering to the warrior ethic.

Defense through reality mapping is defense through anticipation of the behavior of others and the expectation of your own expanded capabilities. If your reality map includes a solution to a problem, no matter how long-term or complex—or the countering measures to a perceived threat—don't hesitate to begin implementing those procedures now, in the real world. Hold to your timetable. Reality mapping delivers incremental progress toward increasingly clarified goals.

Defense through intuitive decision making is defense through detection and countermeasure. We have told you how intuition has saved lives and careers. Listen to what your heart tells you. Never shut out your intuition. It is your link to the warrior's edge.

Defense through visualization allows you to use threat analysis to determine the nature of a problem, and to mentally war-game a solution before you implement it. If you use visualization to construct a defense against a perceived threat, make sure you pay close attention to what you "see." If the image that you see is frightening but it keeps returning despite your attempts to change it into a more benign vision, then your mind is trying to tell you something. Act on that information. The warrior spirit is useless without the warrior's actions.

Self-Tests: Pushing the Envelope of Human Performance

Defense *by* remote viewing is only for those who are unafraid to see what they might not wish to see. We have shown you that the future is no barrier to remote viewers. The warrior is not afraid to learn what he must to be prepared for the worst.

Defense *from* remote viewing involves applying security measures to your home, to your workplace, to the information you carry in your mind. You can use your success space to construct mental barriers to keep out other remote viewers.

Defense through mind/body integration means protecting yourself against extraordinary physical and mental stresses. Use human optimization techniques such as biofeedback and the martial arts. Extreme situations demand extreme measures; use intervention techniques only when they are clearly required to save lives. Resolve conflicts *within the structure of existing law*. To fight physical illness using mind/body integration, work in concert with health professionals. To defend against illness and weakness of all types, use the strength-building techniques we have offered. Visualize yourself in your success space exactly as you wish to be. Use your reality map to make sure you are wishing for the most you can reasonably expect from yourself.

When we began teaching you about your belief-system tree, we started at the root level. We hope we have given you the impetus to expand your beliefs at the root level. We hope you use this book as a primer, a guide that allows you to chart a new reality map of your life.

The life of a nation is no better than the lives of its citizens. All people crave freedom, as conflicts and their resolutions around the world continually remind us. Personal freedom and freedom of thought are intimately linked. So are our minds and the universe, as science is beginning to discover.

With these techniques, you are free to realize your full potential. We hope you will try to do so. We further hope you will be as successful as your wildest dreams.

Nationally and internationally, no less than personally, we

can benefit from wider study and implementation of these techniques. In laboratories around the globe, research continues.

Ultimately, this research goes on in a very special laboratory: the mind and body of a single human being. Warriors throughout history have found the keys to that laboratory and the inexhaustible potential that lies behind its doors. Use the laboratory at your disposal and join us at the warrior's edge.

APPENDIX A

DESCRIPTOR QUERIES

1. Is any significant part of the perceived scene indoors?
2. Is the scene predominantly dark; e.g., poorly lit indoors, nighttime outside, etc. (not simply dark colors, etc.)?
3. Does any significant part of the scene involve perception of height, or depth; e.g., looking up at a tower, tall building, mountain, vaulted ceiling, unusually tall trees, etc., or down into a valley, or down from any elevated position?
4. From the agent's perspective, is the scene well bounded; e.g., interior of a room, a stadium, a courtyard, etc.?
5. Is any significant part of the scene oppressively confined?
6. Is any significant part of the scene hectic, chaotic, congested, or cluttered?
7. Is the scene predominantly colorful, characterized by a profusion of color, or are there outstanding brightly colored objects prominent; e.g., flowers, stained-glass windows, etc. (not normally blue sky, green grass, usual building colors, etc.)?
8. Are any signs, billboards, posters, or pictorial representations prominent in the scene?
9. Is there any significant movement or motion integral to the scene; e.g., a stream of moving vehicles, walking or running people, blowing objects, etc.?
10. Are there any explicit and significant sounds; e.g., auto horns, voices, bird calls, surf noises, etc.?
11. Are any people or figures of people significant in the scene other than the agent or those implicit in buildings, vehicles, etc.?
12. Are any animals, birds, fish, major insects, or figures of these significant in the scene?
13. Does a single major object or structure dominate the scene?
14. Is the central focus of the scene predominantly natural, i.e., not man-made?

Appendix A

15. Is the immediately surrounding environment of the scene predominantly natural, i.e., not man-made?

16. Are any monuments, sculptures, or major ornaments prominent?

17. Are explicit geometric shapes; e.g., triangles, circles, or portions of circles (such as arches), spheres or portions of spheres, etc. (but excluding normal rectangular buildings, doors, windows, etc.) significant in the scene?

18. Are there any posts, poles, or similar thin objects; e.g., columns, lampposts, smokestacks, etc. (excluding trees)?

19. Are doors, gates, or entrances significant in the scene (excluding vehicles)?

20. Are windows or glass significant in the scene (excluding vehicles)?

21. Are any fences, gates, railings, dividers, or scaffolding prominent in the scene?

22. Are steps or stairs prominent (excluding curbs)?

23. Is there regular repetition of some object or shape; e.g., parking lot full of cars, marina with boats, a row of arches, etc.?

24. Are there any planes, boats, or trains, or figures thereof apparent in the scene?

25. Is there any other major equipment in the scene; e.g., tractors, carts, gasoline pumps, etc.?

26. Are there any autos, buses, trucks, bikes, motorcycles, or figures thereof prominent in the scene (excluding agent's car)?

27. Does grass, moss, or similar ground cover compose a significant portion of the surface?

28. Does any central part of the scene contain a road, street, path, bridge, tunnel, railroad tracks, or hallway?

29. Is water a significant part of the scene?

30. Are trees, bushes, or major potted plants apparent in the scene?

APPENDIX B

Signature _____

Date & Time _____

Location _____

Descriptor	Yes	No	Comments	Emph.	Unsure
1. Indoors					
2. Dark					
3. Height					
4. Bounded					
5. Confined					
6. Hectic					
7. Color					
8. Signs					
9. Motion					
10. Sound					
11. People					
12. Animals					
13. Single Object					
14. Natural Focus					
15. Natural Environment					
16. Monuments					
17. Shapes					
18. Poles					
19. Doors					
20. Glass / Windows					
21. Fences					
22. Stairs					
23. Same					
24. Planes					
25. Equipment					
26. Vehicles					
27. Grass					
28. Roads					
29. Water					
30. Trees					

Happy Remote Viewing!

NOTES

CHAPTER 1: BELIEVERS

1. George Leonard, "The Warrior," *Esquire* (July 1986).
2. *Military Leadership*, Headquarters, Department of the Army, Washington, D.C., FM 22-100 (31 October 1983).
3. Leonard, op. cit.
4. Max Planck, *The Universe in the Light of Modern Physics*, trans. W. H. Johnson (New York: W. W. Norton and Co., 1931).
5. R. A. Leeper, "Study of a Neglected Portion of a Field of Learning: The Development of Sensory Organization," *Journal of Genetic Psychology*, Vol. 36 (1935).
6. Elisabeth Kübler-Ross, M.D., *On Death and Dying* (New York: Macmillan, 1969).

CHAPTER 2: MIND CONTROL

1. Some of the journals that have covered this topic include: *The New England Journal of Medicine, Scientific American, Psychosomatic Medicine,* and *Journal of Applied Physiology.*
2. Robert Keith Wallace, Ph.D., and Herbert Bensen, M.D., "The Physiology of Meditation," *Scientific American*, Vol. 226 (1972); Robert Keith Wallace, Ph.D., Herbert Bensen, M.D., and Archie Wilson, M.D., Ph.D., "A Wakeful Hypometabolic Physiologic State," *American Journal of Physiology*, Vol. 221 (1971).
3. O. C. Simonton and S. Simonton, "Belief Systems and Management of the Emotional Aspects of Malignancy," *Journal of Transpersonal Psychology*, Vol. 7, No. 1 (1975).
4. H. I. Russek, "Stress, Tobacco, and Coronary Heart Disease in North American Professional Groups," *Journal of the American Medical Association*, Vol. 192 (1965).

CHAPTER 3: INFLUENCE

1. Captain John D. LaMothe, *Controlled Offensive Behavior—USSR*, Defense Intelligence Agency, Washington, D.C., ST-CS-01-169-72 (July 1972).
2. Ibid.
3. Ibid.
4. Ibid.
5. E. C. Wortz, Ph.D., et al., *Novel Biophysical Transfer Mechanisms (NBIT)*, Final Report, Document No. 76-13197, Government Contract No. X6-4208 (54-20) 75S, AI Research Manufacturing Company of Torrence, California (Torrence, CA: Jan. 14, 1976).
6. James D. Bray, *Questionnaire Results on the Prospects for Soviet Development of Parapsychology for Military or Political Purposes*, Naval Postgraduate School, Monterey, California (December 1978).
7. Ibid.
8. Richard Bandler and John Grinder, *The Structure of Magic* (Palo Alto, Calif.: Science and Behavior, 1975).
9. B. H. Kantowitz and H. L. Roediger III, "Memory and Information Processing," in G. M. Garza and R. J. Corsini, eds., *Theories of Learning* (Itaska, Ill: F. E. Peacock, 1980).
10. Ernest J. McCormick, Ph.D., and Mark S. Sanders, Ph.D., *Human Factors in Engineering and Design*, 5th ed. (New York: McGraw-Hill, 1982).
11. K. Steinbuch, "Information Processing in Man" (Paper presented at IRE International Congress on Human Factors in Electronics, Long Beach, California, May 1962).
12. D. E. Broadbent, *Perception and Communication* (New York: Pergamon Press, 1958); and D. E. Broadbent, *Decision and Stress* (New York: Academic Press, 1971).
13. Ferrel G. Stremler, *Introduction to Communication Systems*, 2nd ed. (Reading, Mass.: Addison-Wesley, 1982).
14. B. H. Deatherage, "Auditory and Other Sensory Forms of Information Processing," in H. P. Van Cott and R. G. Kinkade, eds., *Human Engineering Guide to Equipment Design*, rev. ed. (Washington, D.C.: U.S. Government Printing Office, 1972).
15. McCormick and Sanders, op. cit.
16. James G. Miller, *Living Systems* (New York: McGraw-Hill, 1977).

CHAPTER 4: THE JEDI PROJECT

1. Frederick S. Hillier and Gerald J. Lieberman, *Operations Research*, 2nd ed. (San Francisco: Holden-Day, Inc., 1974).

2. Michael Harner, *The Way of the Shaman* (New York: Bantam, 1980).

CHAPTER 5: CHARTING COURSES

1. Carl Gustav Jung, *Synchronicity*, trans. R.F.C. Hull (Princeton, N.J.: Princeton University Press, 1973).
2. Ibid.
3. Ibid.
4. I. M. Kogan, *The Information Theory Aspect of Telepathy* (text of speech delivered at UCLA, June 1969, based on materials published in *Radiotekhnika*, Vols. 21–23); Captain John D. LaMothe, *Controlled Offensive Behavior—USSR*, Defense Intelligence Agency, Washington D.C., ST-CS-01-169-72 (July 1972); Captain Richard Groller, "Soviet Psychotronics—a State of Mind," *Military Intelligence*, Vol. 12 No. 4 (October–December 1986), pp. 18–21, 58; Captain Richard Groller, "Soviet Psychotronics—a Closer Look," *Military Intelligence*, PB 34-87-1 (Test) (March 1987) pp. 43–44.
5. Paul Davies, *Other Worlds* (New York: Simon and Schuster, 1980).
6. David Bohm, *Wholeness and the Implicate Order* (London: Routledge & Kegan Paul, 1980).
7. John S. Bell, *Physics*, Vol. 1, No. 195 (1964).

CHAPTER 6: A STILL SMALL VOICE

1. Elisabeth Kübler-Ross, *Working It Through* (New York: MacMillan, 1982). Kübler-Ross uses these drawings both as an introductory exercise at her Life, Death, and Transition workshops and as diagnostic tools. The process was developed by Susan Bach while working in a Zurich hospital. Kübler-Ross and others have employed the technique in the United States and have begun to write about it in English.
2. Arthur J. Deikman, "Mystical Intuition," *New Realities*, Vol. VII, No. 5 (May/June 1987).
3. Ibid.
4. Ibid.
5. Philip Goldberg, *The Intuitive Edge* (Los Angeles: Jeremy P. Tarcher, 1983).
6. Andrew Weil, *The Natural Mind* (Boston: Houghton Mifflin, 1972).
7. Roy Rowan, "The Eureka Factor," *Usair*, Vol. IX, No. II (February 1987).
8. Silvano Arieti, *Creativity: The Magic Synthesis* (New York: Basic Books, 1976).
9. Abraham H. Maslow, *The Farther Reaches of Human Nature* (New York: Viking, 1971).

10. Deikman, op. cit.
11. Ibid.
12. Michael Hutchison, *Megabrain* (New York: Ballantine, 1986).
13. Stephan A. Schwartz, *The Alexandria Project* (New York: Dell, 1983). Mr. Schwartz also runs the Moebius Group, which is one of the only for-profit organizations employing advanced human technologies such as remote viewing in a business environment.

CHAPTER 7: AS FAR AS THE MIND CAN SEE

1. Michael Hutchison, *Megabrain* (New York: Ballantine, 1986).
2. Ibid.
3. Martin L. Rossman, *Healing Yourself: A Step-by-Step Guide for Better Health Through Imagery* (New York: Walker and Company, 1987).
4. Ibid.
5. Jeanne Achterberg and Frank G. Lawlis, *Imagery and Disease* (Champaign, Ill.: Institute for Personality and Ability Testing, 1978; 1984).
6. Errol R. Korn and Karen Johnson, *Visualization: The Uses of Imagery in the Health Professions* (Homewood, Ill.: Dow Jones-Irwin, 1983).
7. Daniel Druckman and John H. Swets, eds., *Enhancing Human Performance* (Washington D.C.: National Research Council on Behavioral and Social Science and Education, National Academy Press, 1988).

CHAPTER 8: AND NOTHING WILL BE HIDDEN FROM YOU

1. Steven Emerson, "Secret Warriors," *U.S. News And World Report* (March 21, 1988).
2. Ibid.
3. H. E. Puthoff and R. Targ, "A Perceptual Channel for Information Transfer over Kilometer Distances: Historical Perspective and Recent Research," *Proceedings of the IEEE*, Vol. LXIV (March 1976); Harold E. Puthoff and Russell Targ, *Mind-Reach: Scientists Look at Psychic Ability* (New York: Dell, 1977).
4. Puthoff and Targ, *Mind-Reach*.
5. Robert G. Jahn and Brenda J. Dunne, *Margins of Reality: the Role of Consciousness in the Physical World* (New York: Harcourt Brace Jovanovich, 1987).
6. Russell Targ and Keith Harary, "American and Soviet Applications and Investigations of PSI," *Proceedings: Symposium on Applications of Anomalous Phenomena* (November 30–December 1, 1983).
7. Stephan A. Schwartz, *The Alexandria Project* (New York: Dell, 1983).
8. Stephan A. Schwartz, *The Secret Vaults of Time* (New York: Grosset & Dunlap, 1978).

9. Jahn and Dunne, op. cit.

10. Puthoff and Targ, "A Perceptual Channel . . ."; Puthoff and Targ, *Mind-Reach*.

11. Russell Targ and Keith Harary, *The Mind Race: Understanding and Using Psychic Abilities* (New York: Ballantine, 1984); Targ and Harary, "American and Soviet Applications . . ."

12. Jack Houck, *Remote Viewing Experiment Instructions*, private paper (1986).

13. Ingo Swann, *Natural ESP: The ESP Core and Its Raw Characteristics* (New York: Bantam, 1987).

14. Phillip J. Klass, "USAF Tracking RADAR Details Disclosed," *Aviation Week and Space Technology* (October 25, 1976).

15. Universal Transverse Mercator (UTM) projection is a coordinate system used to overlay a numerical grid onto a map, corresponding to specific locations on the ground.

16. Jack Anderson and Dale Van Atta, "U.S. Still in Psychic Research," United Features Syndicate (October 24, 1985).

17. Ronald McRae, *Mind Wars* (New York: St. Martin's, 1984).

18. Mortimer Feinburg and Aaron Levinstein, "How Do You Know When to Rely on Your Intuition," *The Wall Street Journal* (June 21, 1982).

19. Jack Houck, *Associative Remote Viewing*, private publication.

20. Jack Anderson, *The Washington Post* (April 23, 1984).

21. *NBC Magazine with David Brinkley*, National Broadcasting Company, March 13, 1981.

22. Ibid.

23. Robert A. Monroe, *Journeys Out of the Body* (Garden City, N.Y.: Doubleday, 1971).

24. Ibid.

25. Janet Lee Mitchell, *Out-of-Body Experiences* (New York: Ballantine, 1981); Scott D. Rogo, *Leaving the Body* (Englewood Cliffs, N.J.: Prentice-Hall, 1983).

26. Karlis Osis and Donna McCormick, "Kinetic Effects at the Ostensible Location of an Out-of-Body Projection During Perceptual Testing," *The Journal of the American Society for Psychical Research*, Vol. 74 (July 1980).

27. Lieutenant Colonel John B. Alexander, "The New Mental Battlefield: 'Beam Me Up, Spock,'" *Military Review*, Vol. XL, No. 12 (Dec. 1980).

CHAPTER 9: ACCESSING POWER

1. Pat Tarnasky, "Mind-Body Regulation," *Runner's World* magazine (April 1973).

2. Captain Richard Prien and Jim Myers, "Building a Winner—on the Practice Field and Training Field," *Delta Force Concept Paper* (Carlisle Barracks, Pa.: Army Delta Force, May 1982).

3. Ibid.

4. Martha Davis, Ph.D., and Matthew McKay, Ph.D., and Elizabeth Robbins Eshelman, M.S.W., *The Relaxation and Stress Reduction Workbook* (Oakland, Calif.: New Harbinger Publishing, April 1982).

5. Dan Millman, *The Warrior Athlete: Body, Mind and Spirit* (Walpole, N.H.: Stillpoint Publishing, 1979).

6. John F. Thie, D.C., *Touch for Health* (Pasadena, Calif.: T. H. Publishers, 1987).

7. Frank Mahony, "Are You Sure That's Cross-Crawls?" *Touch for Health International Journal* (July 1986).

8. Steven Rochlitz, "Heart and Brain Integration: A New, Unified Approach," *Touch for Health International Journal* (July 1986).

9. David Shannahoff-Khalsa, et al., "Nasal Airflow Asymmetries and Human Performance," *Biological Psychology*, No. 23 (1986).

10. Deborah A. Werntz, et al., "Alternating Cerebral Hemispheric Activity and the Lateralization of Autonomic Nervous Function," *Human Neurobiology* (Spring 1983).

11. David Shannahoff-Khalsa, *Advanced Neuropsychological Technology Programs*, unpublished (1988).

12. Ibid.

13. Ibid.

14. Swami Vishnu-devananda, *The Complete Illustrated Book of Yoga* (New York: Harmony Books, 1988).

15. Ibid.

16. Walter Reed Army Institute for Research, *Jet Lag Countermeasures*, Walter Reed Army Medical Center, Washington D.C., adapted from handouts for troops deploying on long flights.

17. F. Holmes Atwater, *The Monroe Institute's Hemi-Sync Process* (Faber, Va.: Monroe Institute, undated).

18. Ibid.

19. Thie, op. cit.

20. Ibid.

CHAPTER 10: BIOFEEDBACK

1. D. J. De Witt, "Cognitive and Biofeedback Training for Stress Reduction with University Athletes," *Journal of Sport Psychology*, Vol. 2 (1980).

2. F. S. Daniels and D. M. Landers, "Biofeedback and Shooting Performance: A Test of Disregulation and System Theory," *Journal of Sport Psychology*, Vol. 4 (1981).

3. Daniel Druckman and John H. Swets, eds., *Enhancing Human Performance* (Washington D.C.: National Research Council on Behavioral and Social Science and Education, National Academy Press, 1988).

4. A. W. Hayduk, "The Persistence and Transfer of Voluntary Hand Warming in Natural and Laboratory Cold Setting After One Year," *Biofeedback and Self Regulation*, Vol. 7 (1982); Michael Hutchison, *Megabrain* (New York: Ballantine, 1986).

5. Hayduk, op. cit., pp. 49–52.

6. Johann Schultz and Wolfgang Luthe, *Autogenic Therapy*, Vol. 1 (of *Autogenic Methods*) (New York: Grune and Stratton, 1969).

7. P. S. Coning and W. B. Toscano, "The Relationship of Motion Sickness Susceptibility to Learned Autonomic Control for Symptom Suppression," *Aviation, Space, and Environmental Medicine*, Vol. 53, No. 6 (1982).

8. Hutchison, op. cit., pp. 319–323.

9. James V. Hardt. The bulk of material on advanced EEG biofeedback was provided to John Alexander by Jim Hardt in private communication.

10. V. A. Flugel, "The EEG During Treatment of Hypoxic and Other Cerebral Disorders by Improvement of the Blood Supply," *Journal of Electroencephalography and Clinical Neurophysiology*, Vol. 23, No. 4 (1967).

11. M. Raskin, G. Johnson, and J. W. Roadestvedt, "Chronic Anxiety Treated by Biofeedback—Reduced Muscle Relaxation," *Psychiatry*, Vol. 28 (1973).

12. James V. Hardt. Provided to John Alexander by Jim Hardt in private communication.

Chapter 11: The Absolute Warrior

1. Koichi Tohei, *Ki in Daily Life* (Tokyo: Ki No Kenyukai K. Q., 1978).

2. Ibid.

3. Ibid.

4. Ibid.

5. Ibid.

6. Master Sergeant Henry Slomanski was an instructor at the 101st Airborne Division Jump School in 1958 and 1959, when then Sergeant Alexander was a new instructor at the school. The accounts of Henry Slomanski's accomplishments were frequently recounted.

7. Morley Safer, *60 Minutes*, CBS News, March 19, 1989.

8. Tohei, op. cit.

9. Chaplain (Lieutenant Colonel) Randolph G. "Grady" Spry served as chaplain for 1st Brigade, 25th Infantry Division, during 1976 and 1977, when then Major Alexander was assigned as the brigade adjutant. Both became interested in aikido after watching a demonstration in Honolulu by Koichi Tohei.

10. First Lieutenant Richard Haake served as executive officer to then Captain Alexander, who commanded A Company, 1st Battalion, 21st Infantry, stationed at Schofield Barracks, Hawaii. Rich Haake had studied aikido for most of his life, and passed some of the information on to Alexander.

11. Guy Savelli has been tested at Duke University, the Mind Science Foundation, JFK University, and the Psychical Research Institute. Results of those studies were published in the *Journal of Parapsychology* and in *Research in Parapsychology* (Metuchen, N.J.: Scarecrow Press, 1985).

12. Sheila Ostrander and Lynn Schroeder, *Psychic Discoveries Behind the Iron Curtain* (New York: Bantam, 1971).

CHAPTER 12: SELF-TESTS

1. Robert G. Jahn, "The Persistent Paradox of Psychic Phenomena: An Engineering Perspective," *Proceedings of the IEEE*, Vol. 70, No. 2 (February 1982).

2. Robert G. Jahn and Brenda J. Dunne, *Margins of Reality* (New York: Harcourt Brace Jovanovich, 1987).

3. This comment was made in open session at the annual meeting of the Society for Scientific Exploration (SSE) held July 1988 at Cornell University in Ithaca, New York. John Alexander and many others were in attendance for that session, at which both Sagan and Jahn were featured speakers.

4. This report is based on a personal visit by John Alexander with Edward Kelley and Ross Dunseath, who were then at the Department of Electrical Engineering, Duke University.

5. Jack Houck, "PK Party History," *Psi Research*, Vol. 3, No. 1 (February 1984).

6. Jack Houck, *PK Party Format*, unpublished paper (March 1982).

7. This incident was observed by John Alexander, Major General A. N. Stubblebine, Captain Joe Dick, U.S. Navy, Dr. Andrija Puharich, and many others.

8. Larissa Vilenskaya immigrated to Israel and then to the United States from the Soviet Union, bringing with her a wealth of knowledge of

Soviet psychic research. In the United States, she has published many articles and edited a journal, *PSI Research*, covering worldwide research. She has shown many people, including John Alexander, pictures taken in Russia of macro-PK events.

9. John D. LaMothe, *Controlled Offensive Behavior—USSR*, Defense Intelligence Agency, Washington D.C., ST-CS-01-169-72 (July 1972).

10. Louis F. Maire and J. D. LaMothe, *Soviet and Czechoslovakian Parapsychology Research*, Defense Intelligence Agency, Washington D.C., DST-1810S-387-75 (September 1975).

11. John B. Hasted, "Paranormal Metal Bending," *The Iceland Papers: Selected Papers on Experimental and Theoretical Research on the Physics of Consciousness*, ed. Andrija Puharich, M.D., LL.D. (Amherst, Wis.: Research Associates, 1979).

12. Jack Houck, "Surface Change During Warm-Forming," *Archaeus*, Vol. 2, No. 1 (Fall 1984); Sasaki Shigemi, Ochi Yasuo, and Tataoka Akihira, "Some Observations with Scanning Electron Microscope (SEM) of the Fracture Surface of Metals Fractured by Psychokinesis," *Japan PS Society Journal*, Vol. 2, No. 2 (March 1978). All are from Denki-Tsushin University.

13. Severin Dahlen, "Remote Annealing of High Carbon Steel Parts," *Archaeus*, Vol. 3 (Summer 1985).

14. Jearl Walker, "The Amateur Scientist," *Scientific American* (August 1977).

15. Walker, op. cit.; Jack Houck, "A Conceptual Model of Paranormal Phenomena, Information Transfer and Mind-Brain Interaction," *1985 Conference Proceedings, U.S. Psychotronics Association*, 1985.

16. James McClenon, "Fire Walking at Mount Takao," *Archaeus*, Vol. 1, No. 1 (Winter 1983); Dennis Stillings, "Observations on Firewalking," *PSI Research*, Vol. 4, No. 2 (June 1985). Note: "Explanologists" was taken from this article.

17. Julianne Blake, "Attribution of Power and the Transformation of Fear: An Empirical Study of Firewalking," *PSI Research*, Vol. 4, No. 2 (June 1985). A summary of a doctoral dissertation in clinical psychology.

18. Jack Houck, "A Conceptual Model . . ."

19. James McClenon, Ph.D., "A Comment on Fire Walking," *PSI Research*, Vol. 3, No. 2 (June 1984).

20. Blake, op. cit.

INDEX